DEDICATION

To the freedom of economic acts between consenting adults; and to all Guerrilla Capitalists everywhere.

"To seek the redress of grievances by going to law, is like sheep running for shelter to a bramble bush."

— *Dilwyn*

"Men seldom, or rather never for a length of time, and deliberately, rebel against anything that does not deserve rebelling against."

— *Carlyle*

"That government is best which governs least."

— *Jefferson*

GUERRILLA CAPITALISM

How To Practice Free Enterprise
In An Unfree Economy

ADAM CASH

Loompanics Unlimited
Port Townsend, Washington

Published by:
Loompanics Unlimited
PO Box 1197
Port Townsend, WA 98368

Typesetting and Layout by Patrick Michael
Cover by Kevin Martin

ISBN 0-915179-16-4
Library of Congress Catalog Card Number 84-81910

Contents

1

Introduction

Since 1960, spending by the U.S. government has risen more than 775 percent. The average American worker today pays 45 percent of his income in taxes of one sort or another — feudal serfs only paid about 25 percent of their production to their masters. Small wonder that Americans are "mad as hell" and are looking for ways to not "take it" any longer.

There is a tax revolt going on in America — a double barrelled tax revolt. One barrel is the aboveground tax protestors: those who challenge the the constitutionality of the income tax in court, who file Fifth Amendment returns, argue the Money Question, etc. These people openly defy the U.S. government and fight taxes in the government courts. They get more followers every year, and have the tax collectors worried. But not as worried as the other barrel of the American tax revolt.

The other side is the underground economy — the people we call "Guerrilla Capitalists." These people don't bother to petition the government for redress of their grievances — why should they, when it is the government itself who has grieved them? These people just simply don't pay taxes. They don't file returns. If they file returns, they falsify the returns. The government calls these people "cheaters," but who is being cheated?

1

Is it "cheating" for a person to want to keep the fruits of his own labor? Is it "cheating" for a person to think he can better spend his own money than a bunch of politicians and bureaucrats? It is the *government* who really cheats.

Let us consider the composition of the government which taxes us. Popular mythology says that it consists of "representatives" elected by a "majority." But is this really so? Actually, nothing could be farther from the truth.

Government consists for the most part of politically appointed bureaucrats, a class of tax-consuming parasites who have never been elected to anything. It is the entrenched bureaucracy who really runs things in Washington, and they don't "represent" anything except their own interests. Even those "elected" by "majority vote" can claim no real mandate. Only half the population of the country is eligible to vote. Less than half the eligible voters turn out for most elections. So a politician winning with 50% of the "vote" can claim to be "representing" 12½% of the people, at best. When you subtract out those who voted for him as merely the lesser of two evils, there is no politician in the country who can legitimately claim the "support" of more than 10% of his "constituents." Some "mandate," huh?

Small wonder that people are taking the situation into their own hands, rather than waiting for "reforms" from "elected" officials who represent nobody.

This book is about the underground ecomony — it is about the Guerrilla Capitalists who have simply quit paying all or part of their taxes. It is not about the aboveground tax protestors. It is not about drug dealers, loan sharks, or others who evade taxes on *illegal* activities. The Guerrilla Capitalist does nothing that is illegal in and of itself. He runs afoul of the law only in the area of taxes and licenses.

The Guerrilla Capitalist can be anyone. It could be your babysitter or your dentist. It could be the waitress in the coffee shop where you have breakfast, or the guy who picks up your trash. It could even be you...

2

In this book, we cover in vast detail the whole phenomenon of Guerrilla Capitalism. We consider what types of businesses are best suited for the Guerrilla Capitalist, and discuss ways in which practicing Guerrilla Capitalists evade taxes. Dozens of capsule descriptions of actual underground businesses are given, along with three chapter-length "case histories," which lead you step-by-step through the day-to-day business of the underground economy.

We will discuss the trouble with banks, and how the Guerrilla Capitalist avoids them. We show you how Guerrilla Capitalists "fiddle" the books, how they falsify tax returns, and what they do with their unreported income. We cover how the IRS can discover unreported income, and what Guerrilla Capitalists can do to protect themselves from the IRS. And we provide plenty of sources for further information.

Of course, neither the author nor the publisher advocates tax evasion or the breaking of any law. The purpose of this book is to show what Americans are doing to reduce taxes *on their own,* without waiting for their "representatives" to "help" them. When governments develop the maturity to allow freedom of economic acts among consenting adults, there will be no more underground economy. But until then, the underground economy exists, and it is the domain of the Guerrilla Capitalist, whose ranks are growing steadily.

2

Taxes, Taxes and More Taxes

In theory, taxes are the price citizens pay for living in a civilized society. As originally laid out by the Constitution, the federal government was empowered to collect certain excise taxes to support its minimal activities.

The world has changed since the Constitution was ratified. Governments in general, not only our own, have gotten bigger, and now intrude into areas of our lives that were left alone in bygone years. The phrase "big government" has come into common usage.

Big government requires big money to support it. It gets this money by taxation. In some countries, the official tax rate is nothing less than fierce. In Israel, the government calculated that its citizens were paying 71 percent of their gross income in taxes.[1]

Governments are greedy. This sounds sacrilegious to those who have a worshipful attitude toward the government, but it is true, for the simplest of reasons. Big government is run by small men — such uninspiring figures as Jimmy Carter, Spiro Agnew, and Margaret Thatcher — politicians who promise much and deliver little.

Some people have great respect for the law. While laws may be necessary for the smooth running of a society, it is important to remember that laws are made by men, and are therefore as imperfect as the men who make them.

Tax laws are even more silly and incomprehensible than other laws. While most of us understand and recognize the need for laws against acts such as murder, robbery, and the like, it is hard to see the wisdom in a law that taxes the residents of one state at one rate, while the residents of another pay a different rate. It is also difficult to see why liquor and cigarettes are taxed at different rates in different states.

It is galling to see a millionaire, who gets his income from tax-free bonds, pay less in taxes than his chauffeur, whose income is salary and reported on a W-2 form to the IRS.

The tax parasites try to inspire a feeling of guilt in the person who evades paying taxes by telling him that his "share" will have to be paid by someone else. That is just so much baloney. In the first place, it assumes that the government has some kind of right to spend as much as they possibly can, and then it is up to the rest of us to pay "our share" of *their* debts. In this country, the government is supposed to be the servant of the people, and therefore should be willing to get by on whatever the people voluntarily provide. In the second place, just because one guy doesn't pay his taxes doesn't mean that some other guy has to pay more. Just the opposite could be the case. During the War Between the States, Lincoln imposed the first federal income tax. So few people paid it that the government had to abandon it. So we see that, contrary to government propaganda, people who don't pay their "share" can actually cause everybody's taxes to be reduced.

And in the third place, what exactly is everybody's "fair share"? According to the National Taxpayers Union,[2] the individual taxpayer's share of the trillion dollar debt "our" politicians have run up is $116,125. This is for the public debt alone. Adding in accounts payable, undelivered orders, long-term contracts, loan and credit guarantees, and other commitments and obligations, we get a bill for $148,653 for your "fair share" of 1982's federal government expenditures. Most of the readers of this book probably didn't make that much in any recent year. The point here is that there is simply no way the national debt can be paid off, and anyone who whines that Guerrilla Capitalists are not paying their "fair share" is simply full of bad smelling material.

Dan Bawly, Isreali accountant and commentator, takes the view that **big government** and big taxes are evils in themselves.[3] Jerome Tuccille[4] points out that high taxes serve as an incentive to evasion, and that low tax rates are not worth the trouble of evading. He supports his case by citing the examples of West Germany and Japan, which, in the post-war era, dropped their tax rates and consequently had few problems with tax evasion.

It is common sense that people will make great efforts to evade burdensome taxes. Where the taxes are light, it is simply not worth the trouble.

NOTES

1. *The Subterranean Economy,* Dan Bawly, McGraw-Hill, 1982. p. 1.
2. National Taxpayers Union, 325 Pennsylvania Ave, SE, Washington, DC 20003.
3. Bawly, *op. cit.,* pp. 35-46.
4. *Inside the Underground Economy,* Jerome Tuccille, New American Library, 1982, pp. 125-126.

3

How Big Is
The Underground Economy?

How big is the Underground Economy? Nobody knows.
That's it, in two words.

There have been scores of magazine articles published on
this point, and at least a dozen books, but they are all based
on estimates which disagree with each other by as much as
tenfold, and may be even further away from the real figure.

Senator Lloyd Bentsen[1] mentioned a figure of $700 billion,
one third of the gross national product. Jerome Kurtz,
former IRS Commissioner, claims that between $75 and
$100 billion was not reported in 1976.[2] Professor Edgar
Feige claims that the underground economy was $542 billion
in 1978.[3] This estimate is contradicted by James S. Henry,[4]
who claims that Feige's method was inaccurate. Dan Bawly,
Israeli accountant, takes the most intelligent view of all and
states flatly that there are serious inaccuracies in the
estimates of the size of the underground economy.[5]

From the various estimates given, several trends stand
out. The IRS tends to make low estimates because of its
official line that the tax system in the United States is just
and fair, and most people comply with it. "Voluntary
Compliance" is the basis of tax collection by the IRS, but
even Commissioner Kurtz admits that revenue is lower
where income is self-reported and there is no withholding.[6]

To admit that most people evade taxes would open up a Pandora's box for the IRS, which is why they turn away from the higher estimates. In any event, who can prove them wrong?

There are basically two ways of measuring the size of something, whether it be the distance from the Earth to the moon or the size of the underground economy. One is direct measurement, and the other is indirect. Direct measurement is simple and straightforward. It is possible to measure declared income and taxes paid by simply totalling the amounts reported on tax returns. Unreported income and unpaid taxes, on the other hand, can only be estimated. It is not practical to survey people to ask them how much in taxes they evaded last year.

There are several indirect methods used. One is to count the amount of cash in circulation, multiply it by "velocity," the number of times the average dollar changes hands in a year, and derive an estimate from that. The errors in that method are obvious.

Another indirect method is the "Exact Match File," a closely-held government survey in which tens of thousands of people were questioned by an outside source, to avoid disclosure of IRS involvement, and the data matched with their official tax returns.[7] It is hard to believe people would reveal much irregular income to anyone conducting a survey, and it is very unlikely that big operators, such as drug dealers and gamblers, would answer any questions at all.

Yet another approach, theoretically the most rational one, is a study derived from the 1972-73 Consumer Expenditure Survey of Labor Statistics.[8] The idea behind this method is that, while the supplier of underground services would be reluctant to answer questions, the consumers would not. Accordingly, the reported totals of consumer spending on items such as food, babysitting, etc., were analyzed to try to determine the amounts that went to open suppliers and those that went to informal ones, such as roadside stands and moonlighters. This seems very logical, until a study of each category surveyed[9] reveals that, instead of exact measurements, the paragraphs are filled with words such as "probably," "it was decided to regard ten percent," (who decided and why?) "was treated," "Believed that as much as 25 percent," "It was assumed," "Twenty percent of the residual was assumed," "Five percent was allocated to the informal economy," "treated as payments to the informal sector," etc.

This turns the whole exercise into statistical garbage. Even if the people surveyed answered completely and truthfully — and this is doubtful because most of us don't remember every bag of fruit we buy at a roadside stand, or how much we paid the babysitter last year — without knowing the exact status of the parties who received these payments, it is impossible to be precise about the amount that went into the underground economy.

We must judge the validity of these estimates about the size of the underground economy by two criteria:

1. *Are the estimates consistent with each other?* We have seen that they are not.

2. *Are they consistent with the real facts?* Nobody knows. Only one thing is certain: A lot of people are evading a lot of taxes, and feel they are perfectly justified in doing so.

NOTES

1. Hearings Before the Joint Economic Committee, Congress of the United States, Ninety-Sixth Congress, First Session, November 15, 1979, U.S. Gov't Printing Office, Washington, DC, p. 1.

2. *Ibid.,* p. 8.

3. *Challenge,* Nov/Dec 1979.

4. *Ibid.*

5. *The Subterranean Economy,* Dan Bawly, McGraw-Hill, 1982, pp. 113-115.

6. Joint Hearings, pp. 2-3.

7. Estimates Of Income Unreported On Individual Income Tax Returns, Internal Revenue Service Publication 1104 (9-79,) pp. 58-58.

8. *Ibid.,* pp. 118-133.

9. *Ibid.,* pp. 122-123.

4

Underground Economy People

Sam has his own small business — appliance repair. While most of his income comes from contract work for apartment houses and office buildings, he does some work for individuals. When Sam makes a house call to fix a furnace or repair a refrigerator, he will tell the homeowner, "Look, I got a lot of expenses if I have to run this job through the books. If you just pay me cash, I can do it for 35% less." Usually, people will jump at the chance to save that much, and Sam is glad to get the untraceable cash. Sam reports none of this income, although the expenses for parts, etc., are buried among his on-the-books business. Sam also picks up a little more cash by selling used appliances, which he salvages from his apartment house work. He doesn't report this, either. Sam figures this is the difference between just treading water, and being able to get a little ahead. Plenty of his friends are doing similar things.

Sally and Beth are sisters in their mid-40's. They live in a medium-sized Western city, and have children in their early teens. Their husbands are employed at a local mill. Two years ago, the sisters pooled their savings and started a video rental store. They now have an inventory of over 700 movies to rent. They charge from $2 to $4 per day for each rental. All of this money is in cash. Sally and Beth give receipts when a customer rents a movie, but the receipts are not numbered. At the end of each week, the sisters go through the receipts and throw every other one away, and pocket half of the cash that came in that week. This makes their video store just barely break even on the books, which is OK, because their husbands are both fully employed, and Sally and Beth do not need to show that they are making a living from their business. They take turns running the store themselves, and have no employees to find out their little secret. It is unlikely they will ever be caught.

Harry is a moonlighting Guerrilla Capitalist. He lives in a trailer park in a college town. He owns a modest mobile home and rents a lot, water and sewer from the park. Harry works nights in a local factory, and this is his visible means of support, but Harry is also an underground landlord. Over the years, Harry has purchased four mobile homes in the trailer park where he lives. Harry bought them cheap, fixed them up, and rents them to college students. The trailers are really pretty crummy, but Harry rents them cheap, and knows college students will put up with just about anything. Harry's housing is no worse than most in that college town. Since Harry's tenants are transients, there is a high turnover, but Harry doesn't mind, because sometimes he is able to collect rent from two tenants for the same trailer — e.g., if a tenant pays for the month, and then moves out in two weeks, Harry can rent the trailer to another student for those two weeks, and collect double rent. Harry does just enough repair work to keep his trailers rentable. Most of his "repairs" are made with bailing wire, duct tape and crazy glue. Harry figures if one tenant doesn't like it, he can soon rent the place to another housing-hungry college student. Harry gets his rent in cash. He reports the rent income on one of his units, so that he can deduct all his repair expenses for the other units. The rent from three of his trailers, Harry just pockets. Harry has been doing this for years.

Chuck and Lydia are grad students at a large midwestern university. They help pay the cost of their studies by running an unusual business — they write term papers for undergrads. Through friends in fraternities and sororities, they have set up a little "grapevine" which brings them all the business they can handle. Most of their customers are freshmen and sophomores who are barely hanging on in school, although Chuck and Lydia have both written some papers for upperclassmen. They get paid in cash, and guarantee at least a "C," or else a full refund. They charge an average of $50 per paper. Chuck and Lydia are both intelligent, literate, well read, and experienced in the BS college profs like to hear. When they get an "assignment," they will spend a couple of hours going over the course syllabus, and find out what they can about the prof's prejudices. They then bat out the term paper in about 20 minutes on their word processor. Sometimes, Chuck and Lydia will accept other similiar assignments — book reviews, research projects, etc. They average about 2 assignments each, per week, while school is on. They have never reported any of this income.

Andy is a retired Army sergeant. His pension is enough for him to get by OK, but Andy supplements his income by playing poker. Andy became a good poker player in the service, and has continued his profitable avocation into his civilian life. Andy "works" 3 different games — one that he thinks of as a "major league" game ($10 limit), and two "minor league" games ($1 limit and 50¢ limit). He makes a few bucks in the minor league games, but mostly uses these games as a recruiting ground for his major league game, which is where Andy makes his real money. Andy hosts the weekly major league game at his place about once every two months. The minor league games are played in back rooms around town. Andy knows he is playing as a business, so he is businesslike about his "work." He does not eat or drink while he is playing, and he maintains notebooks with detailed records of his opponents' betting habits and playing idiosyncracies. Of course, the other players would feel taken advantage of if they knew how methodically Andy was taking them week after week. But Andy is careful not to kill any golden geese, and the other players think he is "about even." The truth is, Andy makes about $16,000 a year from the major league game, and another $4,000 or so from the minor league games — all of it in untraceable cash. Needless to say, Andy does not report any of this income on his tax returns.

Jessica is a retired secretary. She has had a hobby of painting and drawing all her life, and now that she is retired, has made a business out of it. She displays her oil paintings at art and craft shows, and at various tourist stores around her town. She sells them for up to $200 each, and sometimes more. She has never reported any of this income. She knows she is supposed to pay taxes on it, but figures her chances of getting caught are small. She knows dozens of other people doing the same thing.

Mindy is a pretty typical teenage girl. After school, and in the summertime, she picks up some money by babysitting for families around the neighborhood. They pay her $3 per hour in cash, and take no taxes out. Mindy does not report this income, even though there have been a couple of years when she made enough to be required to file an income tax return. Mindy is only vaguely aware that she is supposed to be paying tax on her babysitting income — she doesn't really care one way or the other. All her friends are doing the same thing, and none of them have ever been hassled.

Terry is in his late twenties and lives in a large Eastern city. He is laid off from his job as a welder. He draws unemployment insurance from the state. In addition, Terry pumps gas at his brother-in-law's station for $4.00 per hour, cash. He doesn't tell the unemployment bureaucrats about this, since they would immediately cut his benefits. He doesn't report it on his income tax, either. Terry has been laid off before, and each time it happens, he draws unemployment from the state, and works for cash at his brother-in-law's gas station. It is a good deal for his brother-in-law, too, because he gets good honest help at cheap wages.

Garth lives in a middle-sized Western city. He earns his living by repairing watches and speculating in scrap gold. Garth worked for a jeweler for a couple of years, and learned a lot of the tricks of the trade. One thing he learned was that in his town, nobody knew much of anything about repairing old pocket watches. Garth bought a couple of books on the subject, and practiced on broken down old watches from the jewelry store until he felt he was good enough to go on his own. Now the way Garth works it, he has a little "trapline" of jewelers and pawn shops. Every week, Garth runs the line and picks up watches to be repaired, and also purchases whatever scrap gold (old class rings, dental gold, etc.) the shops might have around. Garth also has some coin stores and antique stores on his trapline. All of Garth's customers are glad to have him repair their old pocket watches. They mostly pay him cash and pass the cost of Garth's work on to their own customers. If they give him a check, Garth just takes it to the bank it was drawn on and cashes it. He has been doing business for over five years now, and has never reported a penny of income to the government. Garth doesn't even file tax returns anymore.

5

The Underground Economy
And *You*

Who is the Guerrilla Capitalist, and how does he fit into *your* life?

There are some people in this country who worship the idea of big government, and who believe the government can solve most, if not all, of mankind's problems. In order to do this, the philosophy goes, the government needs to collect massive taxes to pay for its projects. Therefore, being unwilling to pay all of the taxes required is wrong, and unpatriotic. Anyone who does not pay his taxes, in whole or in part, is a criminal. The United States is a country that tolerates, by custom and by law, many shades of political beliefs. These people have a right to their opinions, and those who believe differently have a right to theirs.

Many Americans, while paying their taxes, feel the tax bite is too big, and try to earn some extra dollars in a way the government cannot trace, so they might keep more of what they earn . Americans have a pragmatic approach to life and its problems. Some Americans disagree utterly with the idea of big government and high taxes, and to them it is a matter of principle to *evade* taxes.

Those in favor of high taxes always put the undergrounders in the same category as "criminals." They claim that drug traffickers do not pay taxes, and neither do moonlighters, so they are the same thing. This is simplistic thinking, a refusal to recognize shades of gray, and most people reject this line of reasoning. They know that someone who earns extra money on the side by painting houses on his day off is not legally or morally in the same category as a drug pusher or contract killer. The distinction is both obvious and important.

The criminal is one who commits an act that is illegal in itself, and that most people would consider to be wrong. The undergrounder, or Guerrilla Capitalist, earns his money in a legal and moral way, and his conflict with the law is only on the issue of taxes.

The Guerrilla Capitalist often holds a full-time job, and earns extra money in off-duty hours. You have probably met many of them, without stopping to think about it.

If you have ever purchased fruits and vegetables from a roadside stand, you probably were dealing with a Guerrilla Capitalist who held back some of the yield of his farm to sell outside normal channels, "off the books."

If you have ever hired a babysitter, you probably paid him or her in cash, which almost surely went unreported on any income tax return.

If you have ever been to a nightclub, the members of the band were likely people who worked at regular jobs during the day, and played for cash evenings and on weekends.

Let's look at a few more Guerrilla Capitalists, to get an idea of who they are and how they operate:

Pat is a city firefighter who paints houses on his days off. He has a wife and three children, and often finds it hard to make ends meet on his city paycheck. He needs the extra work to supplement his income, and when he gets paid in cash, he simply does not list it on his tax return, knowing the IRS will be unable to trace it.

Charles is a photographer in a portrait studio, where he earns an hourly wage which is traceable through the W-2

Form he gets every year. On weekends, he has a private practice of his own, taking baby pictures for people who usually pay him cash. He is careful about this, reporting any income which is traceable (paid by check), and does not make excessive mileage deductions on his Form 1040, which might give the IRS a clue as to his actual volume of extra business. He lives in a modest, two-bedroom house which is consistent with his reported income, and is not a high roller or conspicuous spender. He keeps such a low profile that nobody suspects he is a Guerrilla Capitalist.

Clete, a computer specialist, earns a high salary at his above-ground job, and lives a lifestyle consistent with the level of earning. On weekends, he makes high-quality wood furniture in his garage, partly as a hobby, and as a skilled woodworker. He uses the products of his workshop for barter, however, and this gives him a foolproof method of avoiding further taxes. He feels that he is already paying more than his share to support the government, and that he is perfectly entitled to keep something for himself.

All of these people feel that what they are doing is right. Despite the propaganda of the IRS and others, they see themselves as law-abiding citizens who are just violating a technicality of the law. They think of themselves as moral people.

Questions of morality are impossible to answer in a way that everyone will accept. Morality, like the law, varies from place to place and even from person to person. It varies with time. Sexual morality, for example, has undergone a significant change in the Twentieth Century. Each person, moreover, has his or her own code of morality which may or may not be consistent with the law or with a particular religion.

Whether to go into the underground economy, and how far to go, are questions that each of us must answer for ourselves. If you are thinking of doing it, you must be aware that, although many people do it, and successfully, it is technically illegal to evade paying taxes, and you might get caught and be forced to cough up the money the IRS says you owe. There is a possibility of a fine, along with interest on back taxes, and there is a slight chance of criminal prosecution and a prison sentence.

As a start, you need a firm conviction that what you're doing is right and moral, even though it may conflict with the law. You also need the emotional stamina to sustain you for the effort, and the technical know-how to enable you to do it smoothly, elegantly, and without risking discovery. Finally, you must accept that there is a risk, however slight, of getting caught, and having to face reprisals by the government.

If you decide to go into the underground economy, as have many other Americans, you'll be in good company. You'll be one of those free spirits who strives to live his own life, not one of the herd that passively submits to the dictates of the master.

One of the best books for anyone interested in personal freedom and the nuts-and-bolts of attaining it is *How I Found Freedom in an Unfree World,* by Harry Browne, Avon Books, 1973. The author, who a few years before wrote *How You Can Profit From The Coming Devaluation,* an accurately prophetic book about the economic events of the Nixon years, explains his philosophy of freedom. He points out that the government of today does not exist by the enthusiastic consent of the governed, but by their tacit and resigned acceptance. Part I of his book explains why many people are not free, because they accept the traps that have been laid for them, unable to fight back against the emotional and intellectual blackmail that the manipulators practice upon them.

The rest of his book deals with how to attain freedom from the traps, and how to lead an independent life by circumventing both the laws and social conventions.

For those who still have some faith in the wisdom and power of the government, who feel that it may make some mistakes but essentially is running its affairs in the right way, a good book to read is one that is put out by the Treasury Department, and is cited elsewhere in the present work. It is *Estimates of Income Unreported on Individual Income Tax Returns,* IRS Publication 1104(9-79). This is a description of how the IRS tried to estimate the size of the underground economy, and the guesswork and contradictions that went into their estimate. Read it carefully and critically, keeping in mind the amount of time and effort by thousands of people that went into collecting the information summarized in this book, and the uncertainty of the conclusions. The volume does not deal in abstractions, but in dollars, which should be easy to count, but despite this, it fails to present firm conclusions on the amount of tax evasion in this country.

Just as valuable in this regard is the transcript of the hearings before Congress, cited elsewhere herein, on the size of the underground economy. This study, calling upon "experts" from the government and outside it, presents a picture of "experts" running around in circles and contradicting each other. There are many people who have uneasy feelings about the way in which the government runs its business, and this volume will give them much food for thought.

In the "inspirational" category, Chapter Two of *Money Making Secrets of the Millionaires,* by Hal D. Seward, 1972, Parker Publishing Co., tells how some famous men made it. You must be cautious, however, in accepting the idea that all you need is imagination and determination. While these are important, it is also necessary to back them up with technical know-how, and to have a certain amount of luck on your side. It is easy to cite selected examples of success stories, and to ignore all the people with brilliant ideas who lost their shirts because they didn't do their homework or simply had bad luck.

Remember, the underground economy is a boom industry, growing right along with government, and more and more people are taking the plunge into Guerrilla Capitalism.

6

Some Fundamentals

Most successful Guerrilla Capitalists follow a couple of basic guidelines so they can augment their incomes with the fewest complications. These are simple common sense:

1. *Keep a low profile.* Do not brag of your success or your methods. Do not show open defiance of the IRS and don't give them any cause to single you out for special scrutiny.

Part of keeping a low profile is maintaining a visibly modest lifestyle. This means avoiding conspicuous status symbols that advertise the presence of large quantities of money, such as custom license plates, obviously expensive clothing, housing that is conspicuously beyond your alleged means, and other items that can betray the image of an average "working stiff."

There are several common-sense reasons for this. One is, if ever you are audited by the IRS, they will want to know how you can afford a $500,000 house on an income of $20,000 a year.

Another is the risk of informers. Showing off your wealth can provoke envy and spite, two common reasons for informing to the IRS. A neighbor may wonder how you can afford what he cannot, with approximately the same income. If he is the envious type, he may make a call to the IRS. If you boast to him how smart you are in evading taxes, he can give them very specific details that will give their investigation a flying start.

Another motive is revenge. A friend or acquaintance can become an enemy. If he knows much about your business, he can relay this information to the tax authorities and cause you to be investigated.

A third motive is personal profit. The IRS has a system of paying informers up to 10% of the money recovered as a result of information they supply. Some people have so little regard for friendship they will betray their friends and neighbors for thirty pieces of silver. The IRS exploits this "turn in a friend" program as much as they can, and manages to tap untaxed income as a result of information it gets from snitches.

It is important to realize your accountant may betray you this way, as some of them consider this a fringe benefit of their profession. Having access to the intimate details of their clients' financial lives, and the technical knowledge to spot a tax evader, they can easily betray both their professional ethics and their clients' trust.

The main lesson here is not to tell your business to anyone who doesn't have a "need to know." If you have a cash business on the side, your accountant does not need to know about it to make out your tax return. If you and your wife take periodic trips to Las Vegas, there is no need to advertise that fact to your friends and neighbors. You don't have to display your extra income for the world to see.

That leaves you with the problem of what to do with your extra income, and the question: "What good is it if you can't spend it?" We'll cover that thoroughly in a later chapter.

2. The second important point is, *don't get greedy.* You might need a few extra bucks just to get along and keep pace with inflation. It is easy to absorb 10% undeclared income into your lifestyle without making a conspicuous splash and attracting attention. An undeclared income equal to your

legal one is much harder to consume inconspicuously, and in some instances, much harder to cover.

For example, a liquor store owner who "skims" part of his sales, not ringing them up on the cash register, can easily get away with a small percentage of his gross. However, if he tries to skim half or more, it will be harder to cover up. His invoices will show that he purchased a certain quantity of stock, and it will be incredible to the tax auditor that more than a small proportion was lost through breakage and shoplifting.

Overdoing it means taking risks. It requires good judgement to calculate the amount you can safely cover up. Going overboard breaks your low profile and makes you a prime target for the IRS.

7

Starting Up:
The Nuts and Bolts

There are a few basic decisions you have to make before you take in your first payment. If you do not plan, you will be making decisions by default, letting the tide carry you along, possibly in a direction you don't want to go.

The first choice is whether to work out of your home or to have an office or shop. Most likely, you'll work out of your home, but if your business involves manufacturing, or heavy equipment, you may have to buy or rent other premises. There are many ifs, ands, and buts.

Ben runs a small print shop in his garage. He has an A.B. Dick #360, and a Multi 1250W. What he is doing is strictly illegal, in violation of his city's zoning ordinances, but he has gotten away with it for years, since the machinary is not noisy, he works with the garage door closed, and only a few trusted friends and neighbors know of it.

Ann has an electric typewriter and word processor in her home, and operates a typing service in the time she has left over from being a housewife. The equipment is inconspicuous, uses little power, and it has never occurred to her to apply for a business license or check with the city's zoning board.

Frank runs a small business on the side, using his boss's equipment, which saves him the expense of setting up and renting premises. This arrangement is the perfect cover, as he operates under the surface of an already existing, above-board business, only using the equipment after hours.

Setting up an office or shop means more complications. You will be, as far as the licensing and tax authorities are concerned, above ground. Many cities pursue an active, aggressive policy in surveillance of existing businesses, to ensure the city gets its cut in taxes and license fees. Clerks check lists of licensees against the yellow pages of the telephone directory to verify that all businesses have the proper permits and pay taxes. In some cases, city inspectors prowl business parks, office buildings, and other commercial areas to compare the companies physically present against lists of licensees. At least one state makes physical inspections of all businesses, to levy a tax on all the equipment.

Tax and licensing agencies often have cooperative arrangements, exchanging lists of "clients" and other data. The thoroughness of this practice varies widely, as there is a lot of data to process, but it is unwise to assume that you will not be scrutinized to the hilt. For example, if you have a sales tax license you are required to file a periodic return showing your gross receipts and to send the sales taxes you collected along with it. This agency will be happy to provide a copy to the IRS, which means your federal tax return has to be consistent with your local paperwork.

If you need a special license from the city or state, due to the nature of your business, your name will be on a list circulated to other city and state licensing agencies, where clerks will check to ensure you are also on their lists.

There are some subtleties to this that can work against you, if you're not careful. If you use a truck for your business, you'll have to buy license plates from the Motor Vehicle Bureau. A truck, unless it is a small pickup, will usually have commercial plates, and if you have such plates your name will be on a list which most likely will go to other state agencies.

This leads you to another decision — whether to operate totally underground or to skim from an above-ground business. In many cases, it is impossible to operate completely underground, and the proprietor must skim off the top, or conceal part of his income while declaring and paying taxes on the rest. If you decide to skim, you will have to be careful in the way you do it. If you own a bar, liquor store, or other retail business, you'll be dealing in cash, and skimming a proportion of your income will be easy, but you will have to watch your expenses and stock purchases to keep them consistent with the amount of income you'll declare.[1]

If your are moonlighting as a plumber, some customers will pay you in cash and some by check. This makes the decision easy, as you can skim the cash payments. The fact that you already have an above ground job will help conceal the skimming, as you will not have to show the IRS you are earning a living from your moonlighting, as you would if it were your full-time occupation.

If your business is your sole source of income, you obviously have to show you make a living at it, and you can't declare a profit that leaves you too little to subsist. That limits your potential, but brings us back to one of the fundamental rules: *Don't get greedy.* Greed can lead you into a trap of your own making.

You now have to consider another decision, whether to deal in cash or checks. In some types of businesses, as we have seen, the trade will be in cash. In others, you'll often have to take checks. You can limit this by offering some of your customers a discount for cash, which will increase your opportunities for skimming, or you can take a chance and try to conceal the income you get by check.

Tim, a repairman, has a few accounts on the side. His total income from this comes to less than a thousand dollars a year, almost all of it in checks, which he deposits in his bank

31

account. He knows his lifestyle is not exaggerated, and in any event he does not earn enough to spend conspicuously. He also realizes that, although the checks leave a paperwork trail that would betray him under the scrutiny of a full-scale investigation, this is extremely unlikely because his income, lifestyle, and tax return are very ordinary, and not apt to arouse the curiosity of an Internal Revenue Agent. He has gotten away with this for years.

Advertising is another subject for decision. An above-ground business usually must advertise to survive, if only to keep up with the competition. It requires a certain volume of business to stay solvent. As an undergrounder, you are not locked in to a certain amount of business, unless you're in a venture that carries a certain overhead, forcing you to operate at least partially above-ground, as overhead usually comprises rent on premises, license fees, and other expenses not directly tied in with the amount of work you do.

The successful undergrounder usually depends on word-of-mouth advertising. This happens in several ways. One customer can recommend you to another. You can, if your regular job and extra-curricular activities dovetail, do this yourself.

Ben, a former butcher now working as a meat salesman, mentions to some of his accounts that he is available to work a few hours a week, off the books, to help them through their peak periods. As a salesman, his hours are not fixed, and he is able to find the time to work for cash during normal business hours.

Another way to advertise is to "cold canvass," calling on businesses to let them know your services are available. This usually means many unproductive hours, as most prospects will turn you down, but on the other hand, you're looking for only a few accounts.

Sometimes the guerrilla business and the regular job are totally unrelated, yet they dovetail. *Nicholas, a machinist, operates a small coffee and cake concession on his company's premises, with the full approval of management. He earns extra income by selling coffee and rolls to his fellow employees during breaks. He deals only in cash, charges no sales tax, rents no shop or office (he gives the managers free coffee and Danishes in return for being allowed to operate) and does not declare his extra income.*

By planning your business, you'll be able to run it smoothly and avoid awkward and last-minute decisions. You'll also be better able to avoid the risk and embarrassment of getting caught.

NOTES

1. *The Mirage,* Smith and Zekman, Random House, 1979. The chapter titled, "Skimming, Anyone?," pages 175-182, is a primer on the ins and outs of tax avoidance in operating a small business. The techniques explained are in relation to a bar, but are applicable to almost any sort of small operation. The chapter presents the points of view of several experienced accountants who regularly helped their customers to skim profits, and their advice on keeping things in proportion is worth close attention.

8

Moonlighting

"Moonlighting" is a word used to describe either an above-ground second or part-time job, or one that is "off the books." Many people need a second job to make ends meet today, and some find it expedient to make an arrangement to avoid paying income taxes on their second job.

In many instances this is not possible. "Butch," one employer, said: "I just won't do it. If someone works for me I won't do anything illegal to help him avoid paying taxes. It's not worth it to me if I get caught."

Terry, another employer, answered: "I can do it, but it means I have to pay him cash out of my pocket. I have to pay the taxes myself, but I'd do it if I needed someone badly enough."

The difficulty is in the records employers are required to keep, and the cut of the pie the IRS expects to get. To save the employee's having to pay income taxes, the payment must be in cash. Paying by check, on a contract labor basis, avoids withholding taxes but the employee must still report it as income and pay taxes on it, and as banks routinely microfilm all checks, the IRS can find out about the extra income if it investigates.

With all that, your chances of moonlighting in the strict sense, "off the books," are still good, as many employers routinely pay their workers this way. One of the biggest categories is that which employs illegal immigrants. Such labor is typically very inexpensive, and employers take the chance of being discovered and regularly pay in cash.

There are several incentives, not all of them financial, for an employer to pay his hired help in cash:

1. The employer must keep records of payments and of various withholdings on every employee legally employed. This can be a chore, especially if there is high turnover. By paying help "off the books," the employer's record-keeping is simplified.

2. The employer legally must pay more than wages, for all "on the books" employees. He must pay for workman's compensation insurance, make a Social Security payment equal to the employee's contribution, and pay unemployment insurance premiums in most states. This increases his labor costs.

3. Usually, off the books employees don't get the fringe benefits regular employees do. Depending on the company and its benefits, hiring underground labor can save quite a lot in such costs.

4. Because of their underground nature, moonlighting workers are never unionized. Many employers do not like unions, or even the prospect of a union organizing the employees, and hiring the undergrounders avoids this.

5. Many moonlighters demand less in wages than their legal counterparts. Often, they will work extra hours without expecting time and one-half. This saves the employers a significant amount of money. Illegal immigrant labor is a good example.

So far, we have considered only moonlighters working for a company. There are many more who work for themselves, such as the plumber who does extra work on weekends. These moonlighters, although working at their trades, deal with individuals, and often get paid in cash. Sometimes they must accept checks, but that still leaves the cash payments to pocket unreported.

Finding underground work is not quite as straightforward as finding regular employment. It is almost impossible to walk into a company and expect to be paid "off the books," especially if you don't know the people. Usually, you will find underground work through the hidden job market.

It is a fact that many of the jobs filled never pass through an employment agency or the classified pages of a newspaper. Estimates vary, but many people agree the majority of jobs are filled through the hidden job market, which operates by word-of-mouth. In that regard, if you're seeking moonlighting work, it pays to be well-known in your field, as the word will get around and you'll get offers to "make a few bucks on the side."

For the self-employed moonlighter, much valuable trade comes from friends and associates. There are some points to watch, though. *Mark, a technical equipment repairman, does not moonlight in his trade because his employer would consider him to be in competition with him, and would probably accuse him of stealing his accounts. This could have serious repercussions for Mark. James, in a related field, has a legitimate part-time job in the same line as his regular job, and his employer does not mind because James is working for a competitor, rather than being a competitor himself, and the part-time job is in another part of town, with a largely different clientele.*

Often, friends and acquaintances will happily give work to the moonlighter, expecting, and getting, a lower charge. The moonlighting appliance repairman, for example, can afford to charge less than the established companies, as he has almost no overhead. He also finds it profitable to charge less, as he does not have to pay taxes on that income. He might even find it worthwhile to give an additional discount for cash.

The moonlighter cannot advertise, as advertisements are read by government agents, too. The city government is interested in selling a business license to all who do business within the city limits, and both the city and state may collect sales taxes. Often, agencies of the state, federal, and local governments have cooperative agreements, and the moonlighter who finds a city agency pursuing him will soon have state officials and federal agents on his tail, too.

Businessmen who decide to hire underground labor find ways to pay for it without much risk of detection, depending on the exact method they use:

1. Some pay the people out of their own pockets, paying the income taxes themselves, calculating that because the moonlighter works for less, and there are no other expenses connected with his employment, it is cheaper this way.

2. Some use creative methods of accounting, burying the illegal labor costs in with other expenses. The president of one electronic company went so far as to hire prostitutes to entertain his clients, burying the cost under "sales expense."

Normally, it is easy to falsify petty cash slips. False "mileage" reimbursements and various cash register receipts can cover enough petty cash to pay a moonlighter.

3. For the employer who is in a cash business, such as a retailer, it is easy to "skim" part of the receipts to pay for moonlight help. This is the safest method, as it does not leave any sort of paper trail, if properly done. Many do this regularly, as the ethics of business are different from the morality of everyday life, and many businessmen, realizing that their purpose is to make the most profit, see taxes and labor laws only as obstacles to be overcome.

There is no way to gauge accurately how many people moonlight illicitly. The opportunites are so numerous, the chances of detection so small, and the prospect of tax-free income so appealing, that it is a good guess to say "many."

9

Case History:
Bob, The Underground Diamond Dealer

Bob is 33 years old. He works on the production line at the Fisher Body plant in Flint, Michigan. When he got the job, he began to make more money than he could figure what to do with. At least it seemed that way. He got married, and began to live a little. He bought a snowmobile, and spent most winter weekends in northern Michigan. He and his wife vacationed in the Bahamas. Before long, he made a down payment on a big new car. With all the overtime, he was making enough money to pay the rent, buy the car, keep the wife happy, and still have enough left over for season tickets to the minor league hockey team's home games. Life was rosy.

After Bob had been working for five years, the Union went on strike. At first Bob didn't worry. It was true he had no savings, but he'd get strike pay. His wife, Mary, got a job as a cocktail waitress. Sure, it paid less than a quarter what Bob's job at Fisher paid, but along with strike pay they could make ends meet if they cut back. Besides, Flint is a union town: the landlord wasn't about to evict them for being a little short with the rent, and the car dealer wouldn't miss a few payments. Bob would be back at work soon, raking in the bucks like before.

But the strike dragged on. He fell further behind on his car payments and his rent, but so did his buddies. The strike would be over soon, so why worry?

Then one morning he woke up and his car was gone. It had been repossessed. Bob looked at himself, and realized that he had damn little to show for his five years' work. He was deep in debt; he had no source of income except his wife's earnings as a waitress and his paltry strike pay; his wife didn't complain, but he could tell she hated the abuse some of the customers heaped on her.

On the picket line one day, Bob ran into Joe. Joe worked up the assembly line from Bob. But Joe seemed different from the other guys picketing. While the others talked about their financial worries, Joe was silent. While the other guys talked about how the Flint Generals (the local minor league hockey team) was doing, and about how they had sold their season tickets, Joe talked about going to the Detroit Red Wings' home games. How could Joe be able to afford it? Even before the strike, season tickets to the Red Wings had been beyond Bob's budget.

Bob had first met Joe back when he had told his buddies he was getting married. One friend suggested he buy his engagement ring from Joe. "You can save lots of money," he told Bob, "and Joe is an honest guy." Bob met Joe at work one day and asked about a diamond ring. Sure, Joe said, I can fix you up. Joe showed Bob a catalogue of diamond engagement rings. Joe explained that he could sell Bob any of the rings in the catalogue for less than 50% what a jeweler would charge. Bob figured something funny was going on, something probably illegal. He didn't want to buy a stolen ring. But Joe told him he undercut retail jeweler's prices by keeping his overhead low — "no fancy showroom, no fancy advertising." And Joe offered Bob a guarantee: if Bob would pick a ring he liked, Joe would deliver it to him in three weeks. If Bob took the ring to a local jeweler for an appraisal and the jeweler did not value the ring for at least twice Joe's price, Joe would give Bob a full refund.

Bob picked one he liked. Joe said it would cost him $500. A couple of weeks later, Joe gave him the ring. It was brand new and in a plush lined gift box — just like the one Bob had seen in the jeweler's. Bob was a little dubious when he paid for the ring in cash ("I gotta have cash — it keeps the overhead down," Joe said). But Bob's worries ended after he took the ring to the jeweler in the shopping mall. The jeweler examined the ring under his microscope, measured it with some strange looking instruments, and gave Bob a written appraisal saying the ring was worth $1200. The appraisal had cost Bob $60, but he was happy knowing he had gotten a good deal. A few days later, he popped the question to his girl. Mary said "Yes," and since then that ring has sat on the ring finger of her left hand.

Was there a connection between Joe's apparent prosperity and his part-time diamond dealing? Bob wondered. He asked Joe about the diamond business. But Joe just hemmed and hawed and changed the subject.

The strike ended. Bob paid his back rent and bought a used car; his wife quit her waitress job. But Bob remembered what had happened; he vowed to be more careful with his spending and to try to be less dependent on his job at Fisher Body. Never again, he thought, will anyone come in the night and repossess my car. Never again will my wife have to take abuse from any drunk with the price of a beer.

A couple years later, Joe took early retirement. Bob saw an advertisement for a garage sale at Joe's. He went looking for bargains, and found a few. But the best bargain of all was what Joe told him:

"A couple of years ago, you asked me if my diamond business was making me any money. I didn't want to answer then, because I didn't want you to know just how much money I made in my little part time business. And I still won't tell you exactly. Hell, I don't even know how much I made. But I made plenty. I'm retiring and moving to Florida where I won't suffer through the freezing Michigan winters

41

anymore, and I can't see how I could be hurt by competition now. If you are interested in making money dealing in diamonds, I will help you get started."

Bob was interested. He asked questions. "How much money will I need? How long will it take to learn? Doesn't it take years of study to learn about diamonds?"

"You can answer those questions for yourself," said Joe, "next Tuesday by going on a diamond buying trip with me."

"Now hold on, Joe," Bob said, "I can't get enough time off for a trip to the diamond centers like Antwerp, and I sure as hell can't afford the trip."

"I buy diamonds right here in Flint," Joe responded. He agreed to pick up Bob at 10:00 a.m. on Tuesday.

They spent Tuesday driving around Flint, stopping at an odd variety of places: pawnshops mostly, but also coin dealers, flea markets and second-hand goods shops. At each, Joe would ask the owner if he had any diamonds for sale. In most cases, the owner would show Joe a few items, mostly used engagement rings. Joe would take a duplex magnifier out of a leather holder and look at the diamonds. He also pulled a strange-looking instrument from another leather wallet, which he used to measure the stones. In most cases, he would offer the dealer a cash price for the rings. The dealers sometimes haggled a little bit but before Bob and Joe left the shop, the dealer almost always accepted Joe's offer.

By the end of the day, Joe had spent almost $2,000, all in cash taken from a roll in a rubber band he carried in his pants pocket. "It was a good day," Joe told Bob. "The diamonds I bought today have a conservative wholesale value of about $3,000. But by the time I sell them, I will have done far better than that."

Bob was intrigued, and when Joe offered to train him in the business, Bob quickly accepted. Joe told Bob he would charge him $1,500 for his training, but Bob could pay him from his profits, and did not have to pay unless he felt he got his money's worth. "One more thing," said Joe, "I'm leaving for Florida in four weeks. So we will have to begin right away."

"That's OK," Bob responded. "I'll call in sick if I have to. But what will it cost besides your fee? I may not have enough cash."

"I started out with less than $500 cash. Of course, that was a few years ago. Right now, I would say you would have to have $1000 or so. You will need a few tools: a loupe, diamond tweezers, a carbide scribe, a set of diamond gauges, and a diamond wallet. I think you should buy the best, but the best doesn't cost too much. I think you could get by for less than $100. You need a few hundred dollars for inventory, but more would be better.[4]

"I have about $5,000 in savings," Bob responded. "When can I start?"

"There are five things you need to make money at this business," Joe told him. "The basic tool kit — you've already seen most of my diamond tools. Good places to buy diamonds. You have already seen where I buy my diamonds, and if you make the rounds with me for the next couple of weeks, I think you will be able to take over most of my sources. But you should also learn to develop new sources of your own. You need a good place to sell your stones. You already have that: you can sell them at work. You will need cash, like I said before. Lastly, you need some knowledge. Not just knowledge about diamonds, but also about people and how to deal with them."

Bob called home and told his wife not to hold dinner; he would be late. Joe began training Bob that same night. Joe took him to the room in his basement where he did his diamond work. First they put the rings they had bought into Joe's ultrasonic cleaner. "You don't really need this jeweler's model," Joe said over the faint whirring sound the cleaner made. "I used ammonia and an old toothbrush for years. Then I bought a cheap ultrasonic cleaner designed for cleaning false teeth. I got this one a couple of years ago from a jeweler going out of business."

After cleaning the rings, Joe looked to see if any were in nice enough shape to resell as is. None were. "That's usually the case. If the ring is nice enough to resell, the pawnbroker will usually resell it himself. Besides, just about all the rings I get from my dealers are engagement rings. No one wants to buy a used engagement ring, anyway. But once in a while I'll get a nice cocktail ring or pendant or something."

Next Joe showed Bob how he carefully removed the stones from their mountings. Then Joe began to show Bob how to grade the diamonds. "There are really just four factors in evaluating a diamond: its clarity, its color, its carat weight, and its cut." For the next two hours, Joe examined stones through his magnifying loupe and described them to Bob. He pointed out the black carbon included in one stone, and the white "feather" in another. He noted that one stone had a pronounced greenish color, and others had a yellowish hue. They looked at diamonds of various cuts. Joe pointed out that even among brilliant cut stones (the most popular cut) the actual shape varied, and that the variations make a major difference in the brilliance of the diamond. Then Joe showed Bob how he determined the carat weight of a stone. "The only really accurate way is to weigh the stone. But usually a diamond will be offered to you already set in a ring or other mounting, and you have to offer a price based on examining it without removing it." First Joe showed how you can estimate the weight with a small aluminum gauge, punched with holes of varying sizes. By holding the gauge over a diamond, with a little practice, Bob could quickly estimate the weights of mounted stones.

By the time he went home that evening, Bob had practiced evaluating over 50 diamonds from Joe's inventory. He examined them closely, and told Joe what he thought the color, clarity, cut and weight of each diamond was. He was surprised when Joe told him he was already pretty accurate. "Learning how to examine the diamond is probably the easiest part of learning to deal diamonds," Joe said. "But a lot of people think it is the hardest. The idea of examining a diamond and placing a value on it is simply scary to most people. Don't worry about it, and you'll do okay. Anytime you think it's hard, remember that I learned it myself with no one to teach me, and I'm no Albert Einstein."

Bob was really excited when he went home that night. "I have wonderful news," he told Mary. "Joe is teaching me the diamond business. I am going to work as a part-time dealer. If I work hard, Joe says I can earn thousands of dollars a year." Mary didn't like the idea at all, especially when Bob told her that he was going to have to use some of their savings to get started. But Bob's enthusiasm discouraged her from objecting too strenuously. "I can always go back to waitressing," she thought.

Bob put in his shift at the plant for the next few days and went over to Joe's each evening to study his rocks. He examined hundreds of diamonds. He looked at them through his own loupe and measured them with his gauge. He learned to use a Jo-Di gauge, the strange contraption he had seen Joe use when buying diamonds from pawnbrokers. He learned to test a diamond for hardness with a carbide scribe. Joe showed him how to check for flaws hidden beneath the prongs of the setting.

But most of all he listened as Joe told him anecdotes about past deals he had made, and related the importance of developing good contacts with pawnbrokers and other small businesses. Joe told him the techniques which enabled him to quickly convince pawnbrokers he was an expert, and how by earning the confidence of the pawnbroker he was able to get good buys. He told him how he helped supply pawnbrokers who needed diamonds for retail sales, even though it sometimes meant selling a stone for less than its wholesale value. "These guys are your bread and butter," he told Bob. "You gotta keep them happy."

Joe put Bob to work selling diamonds that very first night. He gave Bob two men's diamond rings and told him to wear them to work. He told Bob what he wanted for them. Bob wore them to work, but all they got him were some strange

45

looks from his friends. The next night Bob told Joe that he did not much like wearing a diamond ring in hopes of selling it. "I feel uncomfortable wearing that ring," he said. "Besides, when I bought my engagement ring from you for Mary, I didn't buy a ring you had all made up. Your jeweler made mine. Isn't that a better way to sell diamond rings?"

"It all depends," said Joe. "If a guy is buying an engagement ring, chances are he doesn't want a used ring. You know, women are pretty silly that way. They want their ring to be new, and to last forever, just like their marriage. But with men's rings, it's different. Thank God men are not so sentimental: they would just as soon wear a used ring if the price is right. The same usually holds for women's rings that are worn for ornamentation.

"But most of the diamonds I sell are in 'custom made' rings. It's really the simplest thing in the world to do. I have a catalogue of rings. When the customer picks a style he likes, I order a copy of the ring made from a special kind of wax. I give the wax copy and enough scrap gold to make the ring to a guy who makes jewelry as a hobby. He charges me about $15 per ring to manufacture it. The wax copy costs a couple of dollars, too. But that plus the cost of the gold is all it costs me. Then I select the right diamond and set it in the ring. After I pay for the gold, the wax copy and the manufacturing, and I install a diamond I bought from a pawnbroker, my cost is less than half what the jeweler in the mall pays for an identical ring. That's how I can sell so cheap. And that's also how I get a reputation for doing custom work.

"But you have to wear diamonds for two reasons. First, that's the best way to sell used merchandise. More importantly, its the best form of advertising I can do. Whenever someone says anything about a diamond I am wearing, I explain that I am a dealer in diamonds. Naturally, if the person ever wants to buy a diamond, they come to me. Or if they want to sell a diamond, they come to me."

Two days later Bob sold one of the rings Joe had given him to another worker. It was a big men's pinky ring with a large diamond, which Bob sold for $1,000. Bob realized the diamond was good sized (about 3/4 carat) but of poor quality (it had two carbon spots, was poorly cut and yellowish in color), but it was the sort of ring the jewelry store in the mall would charge $2500 for. He gave the same guarantee that Joe had given him on his engagement ring. The very next day, his buyer told him it had cost him $100 to have it appraised, but the jeweler had valued it at $2700. Joe had made $100 on the deal. "The easiest hundred I ever made," he told Mary.

Over dinner the next evening, Mary asked Bob if she could sell some diamonds for him. He brought her back a cocktail ring, with one half carat stone, and 9 small stones. Joe wanted $850 for it, he told her. A week later, she sold it to a member of her bowling team. She made $250 on the deal, and her attitude toward Bob's ambitions as a diamond dealer began to change.

By the end of the second week, Bob was very tired from all the work he had done studying diamonds. He had learned how to grade and size diamonds. And he had learned what different grades and sizes are worth. He had learned how to sell. But he was still worried about buying diamonds. "It's easy enough for you to buy from your dealers; they already know you and have confidence in you. But I am an unknown quantity."

"I agree it will take time for you to be confident in your dealings with dealers," Joe advised. "And until you are confident yourself, it will be hard for you to gain the confidence of dealers." Joe suggested that Bob get a few days off and he would give one final lesson in buying from dealers.

The following Tuesday, Joe picked up Bob to go "run the trapline" of dealers. Just as they arrived at their first stop, a seedy coin shop, Joe said, "You go in and see what you can do. Tell Jim (the shop's owner) that I am sick. He has seen you with me a couple times; he ought to respond okay to you. Just remember how I act with them."

Bob went in before he had time to worry. He exchanged pleasantries with the dealer, and told him that Joe was sick and had sent him. He had his little kit of diamond tools with him. The coin dealer had only two engagement rings. Bob examined each, while chatting amiably. They were both so filthy with grease and grime that he could not really evaluate then very well. The first ring has a quarter carat stone, which Bob figured was worth about $125 or so. He offered Jim $150 because he was fearful Jim would reject his offer. Jim accepted, and Bob turned to the other stone. It was larger, about a half carat. Bob figured it was worth $350 easily. He offered Jim $300. Jim accepted this offer as well. Bob reached into his pocket (as he had seen Joe do) and pulled out his roll of money. He peeled off four $100 bills and a $50, and gave them to Jim. He put the rings in his diamond wallet and left. In the car he went over the deal with Joe. "You did okay," Joe said, "but you really could have bought that quarter carat for less."

By the end of the day, Bob had visited seven of Joe's regulars. All but one sold him at least a few stones. All seemed happy to see him. They returned to Joe's home and cleaned the day's purchases. They removed all but one diamond from its mounting, graded and sized each stone. Joe complimented Bob on his purchases, and suggested Bob call in sick again tomorrow.

The next morning Joe picked up Bob as usual. He drove onto the expressway and headed out of town. "We're going to try something different today," he announced. "We're going over to Grand Rapids and see what we can buy there."

Upon arriving in Grand Rapids, Joe stopped at a pay phone. He returned in a few minutes with several pages from the Yellow Pages of the phone book. "I cut out the pages for coin dealers, antique dealers, second-hand shops, and pawn brokers. We are going to call on as many of them as we can."

48

As he stopped the car at the first, a slightly grungy pawn shop in a nasty part of town, he announced, "Bob, you are on your own. I will go along as your silent assistant. You make the deal." Bob hadn't expected it, but Joe hadn't led him wrong yet. They entered the shop. In twenty minutes, they were outside again. Bob had only purchased one diamond, but it was a good one, more than a full carat. By day's end, they had visited only six shops. Bob had purchased diamonds at four of them. "Not bad for a beginner," Joe joked.

As they drove back to Flint that evening, Joe talked about his diamond business. It was a good hobby, Joe said. At least it had started as a hobby. But over the years it had reached the point where he made more money dealing in diamonds than at Fisher Body. He had kept his job on the line for two reasons, he said. He had a lot of genuine friends there, whose company he enjoyed and who were good customers for his diamond business. And the full time job helped explain his income. "I have never paid any taxes on my diamond business," he explained, "That's why I do business in cash only. The pawnbrokers are glad to be paid in cash; I think most of them don't pay taxes on the sales to me, either. And my retail customers save so much money that they don't mind the inconvenience."

As they approached the city, he made a surprising announcement. "I've really taught you all I can. The rest will come with experience. It will take time, but I am confident you will do well at this thing. Remember, you will be learning more about diamonds and people as long as you deal."

He was leaving for Tampa that weekend, he said. Bob could pay him his $1500 fee whenever he felt he could. Meanwhile, Bob was on his own.

One day six months later, Joe received a small package with Bob's return address. Inside he found 20 $100 bills, along with a note thanking him for his help, and explaining the extra $500 was in gratitude for Joe's guidance.

It's been five years since Bob became a part-time diamond dealer. When hard times hit the automobile industry in 1980, most of Bob's co-workers panicked. But Bob didn't worry. His diamond business was making him more money than his paycheck. He didn't have to worry about having anything repossessed this time. In fact, he had no worries about money at all. It turned out that he had enough seniority to avoid layoffs, anyway. But he was glad he was now independent of his job, his union, and the company.

Mary has gotten interested in the diamond business as well. She took a course in jewelry casting at a local junior college, and has taken over casting settings for diamonds. She appreciates the extra income and the independence it has brought.

And Joe? He settled into life in a suburb of Tampa. At first, he figured he would sell his diamonds through classified ads. But before long, he had opened a small office and was buying and selling diamonds about 20 hours per week. He still deals in cash, but now he pays "some" taxes.

Why are Joe and Bob able to earn good money by dealing in diamonds? Like entrepreneurs everywhere, *they succeed because they develop a specialized knowledge.* By study and years of trial and error, Joe learned how to deal in diamonds: he learned how to tell a genuine diamond from a fake diamond, how to evaluate diamonds, how to buy diamonds from dealers and from the public, and how to market diamonds. Bob had it easier: he learned from Joe.

This specialized knowledge is a scarce commodity; it is greater than the knowledge possessed by the people Joe deals with. Because their knowledge enables them to more accurately evaluate diamonds than the pawnbrokers who are their major source of supply, they are able to pay those dealers prices high enough to satisfy them. Their knowledge of marketing enables them to resell the diamonds at higher prices still, and make a good profit doing so.

The disparity in knowledge is the key to earning a profit in many businesses. Just as Joe and Bob's superior knowledge enables them to deal profitably in diamonds, superior knowledge of specialized areas enables other people like Joe and Bob to profit from dealing in old cars, rare coins, oriental rugs, or antiques.

But diamonds are a special case. The diamond industry has long attempted to give diamonds an aura of mystery. Indeed, the industry has conspired to keep knowledge of diamonds unavailable to the general public. Even most jewelers have little expertise or useable knowledge about diamonds.

There exist two excellent sources of information for the prospective diamond dealer. The Gemological Institute of America (1735 Stewart Street, Santa Monica, CA 90406) offers a correspondence course, *Diamonds: Production, Marketing, Buying, Grading, Appraising.* The course is probably the best introduction available for the retail jeweler, and is valuable to the part-time diamond dealer as well. A week of laboratory work is included with the course, and graduates are entitled to advertise themselves as "Graduate Gemologists."

An even better source of information for the individual interested in part-time diamond dealing is *Secrets of Diamond Dealing.* It offers comprehensive information needed to deal in diamonds: information on authenticating, grading, and evaluating diamonds, details on pricing diamonds and diamond jewelry at both wholesale and retail, information on marketing, specific information (including brand names and suppliers' addresses) on diamond tools. Its discussion of how to bargain with a pawnbroker is the best I've ever seen; it is useful to anyone who wants to know how to buy anything from a pawnbroker, coin dealer, antique dealer, or stamp dealer. At $75, the handbook is not cheap (although it is cheaper than the GIA course). But the information is valuable enough that it can easily pay for itself very quickly. For the person who seriously wants to deal in diamonds, this book is the place to start. *Secrets of Diamond Dealing* is available from D & G Direct, PO Box 1084, Whitehouse, TX 75791.

10

Flea Markets, Conventions, Shows and Fairs

Good places to see the underground economy in action are the various flea markets, shows, and conventions which occur around most cities on weekends — dozens of unlicensed (or minimally licensed) entrepreneurs buying and selling for untraceable cash.

There are different types of shows you could set up at — basically, the procedure is the same. You rent a table or booth, set up your stuff, and sell to customers attending the show.

Here are some of the kinds of shows you can find:

Flea Markets and Swap Meets. These can be pretty informal affairs, although some of the bigger flea markets are quite well organized by now. Just about anything can be sold at a flea market — knick knacks, antiques, toys, second-hand goods, you name it. Flea markets can be either indoors or outdoors.[1,2,3] Attend a few, and you can begin to get an idea of what to do.

Craft Shows and Art Fairs. Similar to flea markets, except the items for sale are restricted to "arts and crafts" type items. This means anything you can make. If you have a woodworking or metalcasting hobby, you are all set to turn this into a part-time business. If your items catch on, you can make this into a full-time occupation.[4]

Sarah makes silver belt buckles and small jewelry items. She started four years ago as a hobby, and when her friends admired her work so much, she decided to try selling her things at a craft show. She rented a table, and to her surprise, her jewelry went like hotcakes. Eventually, she was able to go into this line of work full-time. Now she works most of the year making her products, and does most of her selling around Christmas at the big craft shows she has learned are best. She has a sales tax license (many craft shows and fairs will not rent her a table without one), but she reports less than half her sales, and pads the expenses so that she pays hardly any tax at all.

Gun Shows. A gun show is just what it sounds like — a show where guns are bought and sold. Gun shows range in size from a dozen or so dealers to the big ones with 200 or more tables. Gun buffs love these shows, because they can see a much greater variety of merchandise than their local sporting goods stores and gun shops can offer, and since there are a large number of dealers competing with each other, prices are often better than store prices. Plus, there is always the just plain fun of looking at all the guns, running into old friends, and making new ones. You don't have to sell guns, either, to set up at a gun show.[5] Accessories such as scopes, slings, magazines, etc., go very well, as does survival gear and army surplus.

Fred runs a survival store. He sells food for long-term storage, camping and emergency gear, books and related items. He does a nice business and earns enough to get by. What makes the difference for Fred is his weekend business in the underground economy. Without that extra untaxed income, Fred just "gets by." With it, he is "comfortable." What he does is this: Most weekends, he leaves his wife in charge of the store, while he loads up the van with stuff experience has taught him moves well at gun shows, and drives to a nearby gun show to set up a table. Fred deducts all his car expenses, meals, and table rent, but reports only one-third of his sales. Once, he was audited by the sales tax people, but Fred just looked the auditor in the eye and told him he seldom did much business at the weekend shows, but felt he had to do it for "promotion." Since all his weekend sales are in cash, there is no way the auditors could prove he sold more than he claimed.

Other Shows, Conventions, Fairs, Etc. There are many other types of shows, conventions, fairs, etc., where a Guerrilla Capitalist can set up and make some cash sales. If you have a hobby, you must know of something like this in your field of interest. Coin shows, stamp shows, knife shows, science fiction conventions,[6] computer fairs... the list goes on and on.

And you don't even have to sell items pertaining to what the show is about — you could set up a food concession, or something similar, which would bring in money at *any* show or convention.

Wherever cash is trading hands, there you can find the underground economy. Flea markets, shows, and conventions are good places for Guerrilla Capitalists.

NOTES

1. *Successful Flea Market Selling,* by Valerie Bohigian, TAB Books, 1981.
2. *Flea Market America,* by Cree McCree, John Muir Publications, 1983.
3. *Flea Market Handbook,* by Robert G. Miner, Main Street Books, 1981.
4. *Success is Not Working For the Pharoah,* by Steve and Cindy Long, Idahome Publications, 1983.
5. *The Complete Guide to Gun Shows,* by Thomas W. Thielen, Loompanics Unlimited, 1980.
6. *The Complete Guide to Science Fiction Conventions,* by Erwin S. Strauss, Loompanics Unlimited, 1983.

11

Garage and Yard Sales

Garage and yard sales are ways of earning money and getting rid of old and unwanted items that are cluttering your home. They are more common in some parts of the country than in others.

Traditionally, a yard sale is a way of getting back some money on unwanted goods. Some people call them "moving sales," which means they are offering for sale items which are not worth transporting to their new home. In principle, they offer these items, usually used, at prices which make them a bargain for anyone who needs them.

As most of the transactions are in cash, and the people do not record the sales or pay sales taxes, yard sales are a strong part of the underground economy. For the Guerrilla Capitalist, they can be a money-making venture.

As a profitable activity, yard sales are distinguished by one outstanding fact: the return per hour of time invested can be very low. This is not necessarily a disadvantage, as many people attend yard sales as a hobby, and do not consider their time wasted if they don't always pick up a bargain or make a profit.

If you are interested in yard sales, your best approach is to consider them as a money-making hobby. Having fun while making a few bucks is definitely worthwhile, although it is not for everyone.

If you want to run a yard sale just to get rid of unwanted items, your approach is very simple. You place an ad, erect signs, mark your prices and display your goods (prices generally are from 5% to 30% of what you paid for the item) and wait for your customers. At the end of the day, you donate whatever you have left to the Salvation Army or Goodwill.

If you are interested in a money-making venture, on the other hand, the procedure is more complicated, although it can be a lot of fun if buying and selling interest you. It is more work, but it doesn't seem like work because your time is your own and you operate according to the schedule that suits you.

Your starting point is to go to many garage sales in your area. You will learn a lot from observing how others run their yard sales:

1. It is important for you to learn the prevailing prices for various items in your area. Yard sales are among the few remaining "free-market" ventures, in which trade is unrestricted by taxes, price controls, subsidies, and other forms of governmental interference. They are also uninfluenced by other factors, such as monopolies and price-fixing, which affect other forms of business. Therefore, you must know your market, in order to make your prices competitive.

People who go to yard sales go to many, and they soon learn what are good prices and when things are overpriced. On the day that you have yours, you'll be competing with all other such sales in your area, and you must not price yourself out of the market.

2. By attending others' sales, you'll learn the general layout and modus operandi of a garage sale. While there are books available on the subject,[1] you need to observe first-hand to learn the fine points. Going to yard sales will also teach you

what the book cannot tell you: what the prevailing practices are, what goods sell quickly, prices, and how much haggling and price negotiation go on in your area. Local conditions are all-important, and no book can tell you what they are where you live.

Observing bargaining tactics is valuable because one day you'll be on the other side of the table and you'll want to be prepared if a potential customer tries to beat you down on price.

3. Scouting for bargains is an obvious purpose. As you are going to look for profits, you need to find merchandise that is available at prices lower than the average in your area, enabling you to buy it and resell it at a profit.

MAKING MONEY
AND MAXIMIZING YOUR SALES

The key to running yard sales as profit-making ventures is to sell items at enough of a profit to make it worthwhile, and to sell enough of them. You have to deal in two dimensions: price and volume. Let's examine the principles involved:

Buy low and sell high. This is the fundamental principle. By looking for items that are underpriced, buying them and reselling them at what the market will bear, you will make a profit on them.

Look for volume-producing items. Fast turnover of items always in demand will generate profits for you. It is better to sell a large quantity of low-priced goods than one or two high-priced, slow-moving items. A lot of this depends on your neighborhood. In a community composed mainly of young families, baby items will be in more demand than they would be among retirees. Paperback books generally sell well everywhere. Learn what sells fast and concentrate on those items.

Price to sell volume. This is a vital point often overlooked by people running garage sales, and cuts heavily into their sales when they neglect it.

You can, for example, price paperback books at 25 cents each, or you can post a sign reading: "BOOKS — 25 CENTS EA. FIVE FOR $1.00." This encourages people to buy quantities instead of individual units. It also tends to avoid price haggling, as it offers a lower price for volume purchases.

Posting the prices conspicuously will encourage sales and avoid wasting your time answering questions. It is true that many people, if they don't see a price, will walk away instead of asking. Failure to post prices will lose sales for you.

Include "ringers" — items you would not normally sell. The logic behind this is direct. You are going to hold a sale anyway. You will be paying for advertising, putting up signs, etc., so including a few extra items will not cost you much in time or effort.

Look over all your possessions with a critical eye. Ask yourself if you would want to sell them if the price were right. Put whatever you decide might sell out on display, and make sure the price is right. Thus, you have a chance of selling a high-priced item along with the others.

Understanding what determines the price someone might pay will enable you to make a good selection and fix a very profitable price. Generally, standard items cannot command a high price. A standard item is one that is generally available in the shops in that area. You cannot price a calculator, or a TV, at more than what a local store charges, and most likely you won't be able to sell it for more than half or one-third the store price. However, a decorative item, such as a wall plaque, an art object, an antique, or a "collector's item," is not subject to a standard price, and many people don't know what such items sell for in other instances. Apart from a few collectors, people buy these items on impulse and desire. Price is secondary.

It is literally true that one person's gold is another's garbage in this field. A non-functioning grandfather clock, with its guts rusted out, is very valuable to someone who thinks of it as an "antique," while a TV set that has a blown picture tube will usually sell for a scrap price. You may have a box full of junk in your garage, filled with old bottle caps or baseball cards, items that have no intrinsic value. If you lay these out at high prices, sooner or later someone will buy them.

One mistake to avoid is buying these from another person in the hope of reselling them, unless you can get them at a scrap price. The odds are the seller is already taking his profit and you'll have a hard time getting more than you paid for them, if you can sell them at all.

Deal in cash. This is the most important point for the Guerrilla Capitalist, and one which is easy to follow in yard sales. Most people come to garage sales with a pocketful of cash and do not offer checks.

We all know that cash is untraceable, and that depositing a check produces a paperwork trail that can haunt you. There is another reason, however, one which you can use to your advantage if anyone offers to pay by check.

Not all checks are good, and a particular check is no better than the person who writes it. If someone offers you a check, you can simply tell him: "Look, I'm just having a yard sale to get rid of some stuff I don't need. I'm not a businessman. I don't want to get involved asking you for your driver's license and all that. Can't you just go to the bank and get the cash, if you really want the item?" This is a way of refusing a check without offending, and the sincere buyer should not be put off by this. You can offer to take a deposit, and hold the item for him, as an accommodation, until he returns with the cash. This may not be until a day or two later, as the best time to have a garage sale is on a weekend, when most banks are closed. With the proliferation of electronic teller machines, however, many people can obtain cash even when

61

the bank offices are closed, and your customer may be back with the money an hour later.

Roadside stands. Similar to garage and yard sales, in that the sale is set up at one's home, is farmers selling produce from roadside stands.[2] You don't even need to be a "farmer" to do this, as all you really need is a rural location and enough room to grow some saleable crops. Many people dispose of the overflow from their gardens and chicken coops in this way, as a drive through the country at harvest time will reveal. Few of them are crazy enough to report this income on their tax returns.

NOTES

1. *How to Make Money with Your Garage Sale*, Ryan Petty, St. Martin's Press, New York, 1981. This is a good basic book on how to run a garage or yard sale, and covers everything you need to know. Many of the points the author covers are elementary, but you'll be surprised, as you make the rounds of yard sales in your locale, at how many people overlook them.

Also worth reading is *Don't Throw it Out — Sell It!* by Joe Sutherland Gould, Prentice-Hall, Inc., 1983, which is a good guide to garage sales, white elephant sales, fund raisers, tag sales, charity thrift shops, flea markets, and second-hand stores.

Another book worth reading is *Flea Market Handbook,* by Robert G. Miner, Main Street Books, Mechanicsburg, PA, 1981. The most valuable parts of this book are chapters seven and eight, dealing with pricing and the interpersonal relations that are a part of the selling. While the garage sale books touch on negotiations, this one goes into much more detail and has many good points about dealing with customers and handling price haggling. The chapter on record-keeping will not be of much value to the Guerrilla Capitalist, but most of the other chapters start from the viewpoint of dealing with people in structured and unstructured buying situations, and this is a valuable skill to have. Although the author deals with buying and selling antiques more than other merchandise, his emphasis on the dynamics of buying and selling is thorough, and applies to handling other merchandise as well.

2. A good book on roadside stands and farmers markets is *Farmers Markets of America: A Renaissance,* by Robert Sommer, Capra Press, 1980.

12

Case History:
Tom, The Underground Trucker

Tom is 27 years old and single. He earns a nice living with his pickup truck and van. What is unusual about Tom's business is that it is all done underground. None of the income from his business ever gets reported.

Tom is a real go-getter, a good Guerrilla Capitalist. He earns up to $50 an hour or even more by working hard and being on the ball. He is always looking for work to do and money to be made.

Tom runs a small classified ad under "Services" in the Sunday paper. His ad reads like this:

> **MOVING, HAULING.** Pickup truck and van available for heavy appliances, house moving, brush piles, junk, whatever your hauling needs. Call Tom 123-4567.

He puts similarly worded ads on the bulletin boards at supermarkets, laundromats, and colleges. This is all the advertising he does, although Tom will also approach real estate agents, building contractors, co-op managers, apartment managers, etc., and leave a small card with his name, phone number, and "HAULING" on it.

This tiny bit of advertising brings Tom all the work he can handle, because Tom keeps his eyes open for other work, and for "junk" items he can salvage and sell. Let's follow Tom through a typical week and watch this Guerrilla Capitalist in action.

Monday. Tom is up at 7 a.m., fixes himself a quick breakfast, and then is off to work. He is meeting a college student at 8 a.m. and helping him move across town. The student and a couple of his buddies are helping, so Tom doesn't need to hire anyone for this job. He is just charging by the hour for the truck and himself. It looks like rain today, so Tom takes the van instead of the pickup. The job is done by noon, and Tom charges $80, which he collects in cash. Also, the student has left behind a box of books and an old sofa. Tom charges an extra $20 to haul these "to the dump." Checking over the items carefully, Tom decides the sofa is too far gone to rescue, and he actually does haul that to the dump. But the box of books he saves to drop off at a used book store for cash. Tom often picks up some nice stuff for free when he helps people move, and often gets paid extra for taking valuable items "to the dump" which he later sells.

Tom grabs a quick lunch, and then goes to his next job, hauling away leaves and brush from a man's property. Tom uses his pickup for this, since it won't matter if this stuff gets wet, and besides, the weather has cleared up now. The job takes two loads, and after the second load is ready to haul away, Tom talks with the man, and makes a deal to do some interior painting on the next rainy day. By keeping his eyes open for extra work like this, Tom earns a lot of extra money. Once, he did some hauling for a guy and wound up painting the entire exterior of the man's house, as well as some additional yard work. The man pays him cash for the hauling, $30 per load for two loads.

By the time Tom gets to the dump, it is 2:30 p.m., and time for one more job. This time it is a contractor who needs a building site cleaned up. Three pickup loads at $30 per load. On this one, Tom doesn't need to pay any dump fees, since he knows a property owner who needs fill. Tom is done by 5 p.m., and the contractor pays him with a check.

Tom has found that most individuals he hauls for will pay him in cash, but when he works for contractors, apartment managers, etc., they usually pay him with a check, since they need to have a record of the expense for their own tax records. Tom prefers untraceable cash, of course, but he knows how to handle checks to keep this income hidden. Tom pockets the check and heads home. Less his gas, dump fees, and related expenses, Tom has cleared over $225 today — all of it untaxed.

Tom checks his answering machine, as he does every night, and returns the calls. He lines up three jobs for Thursday and two for Friday.

Tuesday. Tom has two jobs scheduled for today, both local moves, one at 8 a.m., and one at 10:30 a.m. The first move takes a little longer than planned, and Tom is late starting his second job. He decides to skip lunch to get the work done quicker. He is finished by 1:30 p.m. A bonus for Tom on the second job is that the family had held a garage sale to get rid of unwanted items before they moved, and there was still quite a bit of stuff left over. Since they didn't want it anymore, they paid Tom to haul it to the dump (or wherever he wanted). Tom looks the stuff over, and hauls about half of it to the dump. The rest (some clothes, some useable furniture, and some old toys) he keeps in his garage until he can get around to selling it.

Subtracting out his expenses, Tom has made "only" about $100 today; but remember, he was done by 1:30 in the afternoon. He spends the rest of the day doing some maintenance on his pickup and van. Tom keeps his trucks shipshape, since they are his livelihood. He checks his answering machine and schedules some jobs for next week, and one for the next weekend.

Wednesday. It is raining today, so Tom calls and reschedules the one job he had today for Friday. He goes out to the place he worked on Monday, and does the painting he arranged for. On the way, he stops off at the bank of the contractor he hauled for Monday, and cashes the contractor's check. The bank charges him a $4 fee for cashing a check without having an account there himself, but Tom realizes this is just an expense of keeping underground. By having no bank accounts himself, and cashing all the checks he receives at the banks they are drawn on, Tom keeps his income well hidden.

He finishes the painting by 2:30 p.m., gets paid in cash, and spends the rest of the afternoon going through the past two or three weeks' of accumulated "junk" he has salvaged from hauling jobs. It is a pretty typical assortment, nothing really valuable, but most of it saleable to the right people. Tom makes it a point to know the "right" people — second-hand dealers, flea market dealers, pawn shop owners, etc., so he can easily dispose of the old postcards, books, clothing, furniture, etc., for cash. He makes some calls and gets the stuff ready to move out on the weekend.

He checks his answering machine, returns his calls, and schedules some more jobs for next week.

Thursday. Tom is up early, as usual. He has three jobs today, two moves in the morning, and brush hauling in the afternoon. The moves are easy, one family, and a college student, and Tom acquires a couple more boxes of old postcards and books. By 1:30 p.m., he has finished both jobs, had lunch and is at the old farm to do the brush hauling. There is quite a lot of brush to be hauled, and it takes Tom until past 6 o'clock to carry it all to his friend's landfill. While loading up the brush, Tom notices an old half-fallen-down barn on the property. Tom makes a deal with the owner to tear down the barn. He will be paid in cash, plus he gets to salvage whatever material he can. Tom knows there is a good market for old barn boards in the city — people like to make picture frames out of them, and even panel entire rooms of their houses or businesses.

Tom will have to hire a helper (for cash, naturally) to help him with the barn. He arranges with the owner to do the job in a week or two. Tom figures he can clear at least $400 from salvaging the stuff from the barn — a job that will take him about a day.

Tom often comes across deals like this — one man's junk is another man's treasure. People often don't even know what they have. The best deal Tom ever came upon was a job he took cleaning out an old factory, so it could be remodeled. The new owners considered everything in the building to be junk, and most of it was, winding up at the dump, and in Tom's favorite landfill. But Tom found two spools of platinum wire, which he was able to sell for $2,500 — pretty good, when you consider that he was being paid to haul it away! Tom knows he won't find platinum wire every day, but on every job, he keeps his eyes open for "junk" he can sell.

Friday. Tom has three jobs to do today: the two he had originally scheduled, and the rescheduled job from Wednesday. All three jobs are routine moves, so Tom is done for the day at 3 o'clock. He spends the rest of the day loading his van with the salvage he has accumulated, which he will take around to second-hand stores, etc., tomorrow. He also takes care of his answering machine, and schedules a couple more jobs for next week. Then he calls some used-wood dealers to get prices on wood from the barn he will be tearing down. Tom describes exactly the wood he will have, and pretends that he is looking to buy, in order to get the current retail prices. When Tom advertises his barn wood, he will charge slightly less than the used-wood dealers' prices.

Saturday. Today, Tom takes his salvage stuff on his rounds. Clothing he drops off at a used clothing store, old postcards and other "antique" type items he sells to antique dealers, phonograph records go to a used record store, books to used book stores, furniture to second-hand stores, etc. Tom has about a third of the stuff left over, and this he will haul to the dump next week with one of his other hauling jobs. Altogether, he clears over $100 for the "junk."

He is done by the middle of the afternoon, and takes the rest of the day, and Sunday, off. This week, after expenses, Tom has cleared well over $700 — and he pays taxes on none of it. He averages about the same, week in and week out.

Tom works a little scam to take care of his income tax. He wants to report enough income so that his visible lifestyle is accounted for, but he knows that if he starts putting his trucking business on his income tax returns, he will be calling attention to the fact that he is self-employed in a cash business. Tom prefers to appear as an ordinary wage-earner, who has all his income taxes withheld.

Tom has a cousin in business, and has made an arrangement to give himself a visible means of support. The cousin pays Tom a "salary" for a non-existent job. Tom picks up his paycheck every week, and deposits it in his bank account (this is the only thing he uses his bank account for). Then he withdraws cash from the bank, and kicks it back to his cousin. At the end of the year, his cousin sends Tom a W-2, just like all his employees. So Tom's cousin gets a tax deduction for Tom's "salary" without having to pay anything, and Tom gets a W-2 showing enough income to account for his visible lifestyle, with all taxes withheld. Some years, he even gets a refund.

Tom's cousin's business also has gas and auto expenses, so Tom sells his cousin all his own gas, oil and repair invoices for half-price — in cash. This way, Tom gets reimbursed for some of his expenses, and his cousin gets more "deductions."

Tom started his trucking business part-time while in college, and made the arrangement with his cousin after he had been full-time for two years. Tom has no sign on his truck to indicate that he is doing commercial hauling, and has never bought any kind of license. Tom figures if he is ever "caught" hauling a load, he can always say he is "just helping a friend move."

Tom is an honest man. He works hard for his money, and all his customers are well satisfied. Tom figures he pays enough in indirect taxes (sales tax, gas tax, liquor tax, excise tax, inflation, etc.) to support more than his fair share of bureaucrats. He doesn't feel a bit guilty about not reporting his income. He's the one who hustled to earn it, and he is the one who should get to keep it, is the way Tom the underground trucker looks at it.

If you would like to learn more about the opportunities available in trucking and hauling, underground or otherwise, a good book is *How to Earn $15 to $50 an Hour & More with a Pick-Up Truck or Van,* by Don Lilly, 1982, Darian Books, RD 1, Canal Road, Princeton, New Jersey, 08540.

13

Home Businesses

There are many types of businesses you can operate at home. The variety is so vast that we can examine only a few here, and suggest sources for further information.

You can use your job skills at home, as we have seen in other chapters. A bookkeeper can do the recordkeeping for small businesses in his or her spare time at home, for example. A computer programmer can write programs at home.

Many people have second or even third skills. *Jack, a bookkeeper for a grocery chain, learned gunsmithing in the army, and repairs guns in his home workshop as a sideline.*

Since computers are not only the coming thing, but have already arrived in many fields, let's look at those first. The field is wide-open, and getting wider. If you're into this, you can earn money in many ways, such as writing articles about computers, repairing them, developing and selling both software and hardware, consulting, and teaching, to cover some of the possibilities.

The book, *Making Money with Your Microcomputer*, Robert J. Trasiter and Rich Ingram, TAB Books, 1982, tells in detail many ways in which a person who understands computer technology can earn money in ways other than working for a company.

There are many gun owners in this country, and some of them earn money on the sale and trade of guns. *The Complete Guide to Gun Shows,* by Thomas W. Thielen, Loompanics Unlimited, 1980, is just that. It deals with the economics and practical details of participating in gun shows, both as a seller and as a customer.

For the gun hobbyist, gun shows are mainly fun. The experienced gun nut knows that it is critically important to know the market, to recognize good values. More often, the gun nut who wants to earn money will look in the classified ads and go to garage sales for good gun buys. The gun hobbyist who is interested in speculation will even buy guns in a retail store, as some firearms are so popular they gain in value very quickly. The Ruger Mini-14 is a good example. Several years ago, when a rumor started that Smith & Wesson intended to discontinue manufacture of its small, five-shot revolvers, models such as the "Chief" doubled in price in some parts of the country.

It is often useless to buy guns that are recognized collector's items, as they usually are high-priced. A dealer or middleman already has taken profit on them. On the other hand, if you find one that a homeowner has dug out of his attic and is offering at a garage sale without realizing its value, you can usually make a nice profit.

For those interested in gambling, holding card parties in the home is a profitable sideline. *How to Hustle Home Poker,* by John Fox, Ph.D., GBC Press, 1981, is an operational and technical manual for those who want to run a home poker game for profit.

Another good book on milking home poker games is Frank R. Wallace's *Poker: A Guaranteed Income for Life Using the Advanced Concepts of Poker,* from Warner Books. Literally millions of dollars in untraceable cash changes hands each year over home poker tables, and it is not difficult for a skilled player to do very well for himself.

Many people play a musical instrument. Giving lessons at home is a way to make that skill pay. It is especially worthwhile if your main occupation is not connected with music, since your sideline will be less visible to the IRS.

Fewer people today have sewing skills than before. For those who do, dressmaking and clothing repair at home can be a source of extra income.

Most people have stereo tape systems; many have home video recorders. The lucky person who has two machines and knows how to use them can earn money copying tapes for friends and acquaintances. Duplicating tapes is not much work, just a matter of inserting the cassettes and pushing the buttons. It is technically in violation of the copyright laws, but this is not a serious hazard unless you advertise. Recording companies have investigators who chase down ads to determine the provenances of their materials.

There are miscellaneous opportunities for speculation, which means that in some cases there are sharp and sudden price increases in certain items which the speculator can exploit. For example, certain cities with rapid transit systems use tokens. The fares increase every few years, and the transit authority then sells the same tokens at a higher price. If you live in such a city, New York, for example, you can buy extra tokens. It is usually wise to wait until some time after the last price increase to start building up a stock of tokens. A little research in the public library will disclose the average interval between fare increases and you can judge the proper timing for your purchases by that.

If you build up a stockpile of tokens, one day you'll find that overnight they have increased in value twenty to forty percent. Then you can travel for quite a while at what is in effect a discount rate, or if you've bought a significant surplus, you can take your profit by selling them at a discount to fellow employees or friends and neighbors. This practice has the advantage of not being strictly illegal. If the IRS finds out, though, they'll hit you for taxes. However, this sort of enterprise is virtually untraceable, as it is usually a cash deal all the way.

This sampling of methods of earning money at home is obviously not a complete list. It is not even a layout of the categories. It should serve to stimulate your imagination, and help you find a sideline that will earn you some extra, untraceable income.

Another method of stimulating your imagination is to open the yellow pages and start with "A," working your way through the book. As you scan each business category, ask yourself if you could earn money doing that at home. Also ask yourself if there are any goods or services not being provided, creating a gap which you could fill. Possibly some goods or services are available, but at prices which most people consider excessive. That may mean an opportunity for you, if you can fill that gap. Your skill is what will sell, but your best asset is your immagination.

14

Direct Sales

Direct sales means selling a product directly to the consumer, without a retail store. Some examples are: Amway, Stanley Home Products, Sara Coventry Jewelry, Shaklee, Avon, and the well-known Fuller Brush Company. The traditional method of operation was for a door-to-door salesman, such as the immortal Fuller Brush Man, to work a territory, going from house to house taking orders for products, which he either would deliver from the trunk of his car or bring a week or two later, after he had received his stock from the company.

Conditions change, and today the backbone of direct sales is not the professional salesman, working his way slowly down a residential street, but the part-timer, usually a housewife, who either sells to friends, relatives and neighbors, or has a small "territory" to canvass. Competition from local retailers, who usually offer similar merchandise at a lower price, has hurt direct sales, and few can earn a living at it today. Yet, it is a useful way of making a few extra bucks for the part-timer.

If you are such a part-timer, the system works like this: You buy the products from the company, and resell them to the customer. The basic relationship is that you are the company's customer. You are in business for yourself, not an employee. This gives you certain freedoms, and certain problems. If a customer neglects to pay you, and turns out to be a deadbeat, it's your problem, as the company is only concerned with collecting from you. You'll collect only on commission, as these companies do not pay their salespeople salaries. The commissions are high, going from 25% up to as much as 50%.

You may be dealing with the company directly, ordering from it and making your payment to it, or you may be working through a middleman, who may have a title like "Sales Manager," and who will deliver the merchandise to you and collect payment himself. If so, he is probably earning an "override" on your sales. This means that he either collects a commission from the company on the sales of his dealers, or he buys directly from the company at a discount and resells to you at a lesser discount. Either way, he is making money from your efforts, and this is important to remember, as some of these sales managers take on more authority than they have and try to bully their dealers. Never forget that he needs you as much as you need him. This can be important if you can spend only a limited number of hours selling and he tries to get you to devote more time.

The company usually supplies advertising literature in the form of fliers and catalogs. The prices are set by the company, but, as you're an independent dealer, you are not bound by them. It is usually easier to follow the list prices, but you are able to offer your customers quantity discounts and tie-in sales. You might, for example, offer to sell a customer liquid detergent at ten percent discount if the customer buys a mop. You can also make a "buy three, get one free" offer, which will increase your total sale, even though you do not make the normal margin of profit on all the items.

Usually, the company has certain items on sale. One month it may be air freshener, the next it may be a toilet bowl brush and two cans of toilet bowl cleaner as a package deal. If you feel you can invest a modest sum, it pays to buy extra stock during the sale, as you'll be billed at the normal discount from the sale price, and you can sell the goods at the normal price later and earn a larger margin of profit.

The best part of this sort of affair is that it lends itself very well to the Guerrilla Capitalist. The only paperwork involved is the order form and the company's invoice to you. The company does not send a Form 1099 to the IRS, as it does not pay you anything. You are totally responsible for reporting and paying taxes on your own income. Many choose not to report anything, and they easily get away with it.

In many cases, checks do not pose a problem. You can simply ask your customer to make the check out to the company, and send it in as part of your payment, which avoids the paperwork trail through your bank account.

The ethics of this business are as loose as those of other enterprises, and both the company and dealers often act in ways that are questionable, if not outright illegal. For example, some companies require you to sign an agreement that you will sell only in the territory assigned you, and that you will not handle other companies' products. Any violation can result in immediate termination of the contract, but in practice this hardly ever happens.

Paul, a Fuller Brush man in the "old days" worked not only his territory, but other parcels of real estate as well. When a dealer quit, his territory was a happy hunting ground for Paul, who knew that he would not be reported as he would be if he "pirated" a territory that was being worked by another Fuller Brush man. He was often able to continue pirating when a new dealer came on the scene, as the novice did not know the subtleties, and when a customer would tell him "The Fuller Brush Man was just here," he would assume it was his predecessor.

Paul also sold Avon, despite the stipulation in both contracts. He was very ambitious, and also circumvented the prohibition against pirating by having a small network of part-timers who sold for him. He knew the field manager would often spot-check for violations, and was careful never to be seen in territories assigned to other dealers, instead having his part-timers, who were unknown to the field manager, do the selling for him. Paul got a 45% discount on his billing, and resold to his part-timers at 25% discount, making an override of 20% on what they sold.

If you are considering direct sales, you'll find that the advantages are that you usually need no special skills, except the ability to get along with people, and you can always work out of your home, eliminating the overhead and other bothers. You usually can choose your hours, and often you can choose where you want to work. The drawback is that profits are limited, but you can partly overcome this by selling several lines. Often, you'll find a customer who tells you: "I know your cosmetics are good, but I always use Avon." If you sell Avon as well, you don't lose the sale.

Stocking can be a problem. There are two ways of handling this. One is to order only what you sell, from week to week, and carry no stock at all. Another is to carry some stock, so that you can deliver on the spot and collect your money immediately, thus saving yourself a return trip. You might also choose to buy extra stock on sale items that you know sell well and all year round, so you can get the extra margin of profit when the price reverts to normal. This means you have to find the space to store your stock, and this can be a problem, as some of it is bulky. If you sell cosmetics, the bulk is small in relation to value, but if you're into mops and brooms, they are bulky for the price.

All told, direct sales can serve as a way of making extra, tax-free income, without some of the complications that other businesses have. Direct sales can be a good way of starting out, as the investment is small, and the time required is mostly for you to decide.

15

Making Money
From Your Hobby

There are basically two ways to make money from a hobby — using it as a peg from which to hang additional deductions, and as a totally clandestine means of earning money. Both are in wide use, and each has its virtues and drawbacks.

The first way is sometimes overdone by people who think the IRS is stupid or naive. Calling a hobby a business and taking large deductions will work only for a time. The Internal Revenue Code covers exactly what is allowed in deducting hobbies, and lays down some strict limitations.[1] Generally, a person who raises horses or collects stamps cannot call his hobby a business unless he earns money at it. Declaring a loss for several years running, while claiming deductions, is an old trick and the IRS has seen it many times before.

There is only one way to succeed at deducting your hobby — you must show a profit, and pay taxes on it, in order to make it legitimate and hang deductions on it. It only pays if you are already spending a lot of money on your hobby, not if you have to lay out more money to earn those deductions.

Damon is a gun hobbyist, spending at least a thousand dollars a year on his guns and allied activities. He reasoned that if he took up writing about guns, he would be able to deduct the money he was already spending on his hobby. He did, and has succeeded in selling several gun-related articles a year to magazines, and even having some gun-related books published. The deductions he gets as a result eat up most of the income, but leave him with enough so he is able to show a slight profit each year, making his deductions completely legitimate and above-board.

The second way of earning money from your hobby is to be completely underground. It is like moonlighting, except in this case you are not using your job-related skills, but your hobby. The electronic hobbyist who repairs appliances on the side, for cash or barter, while working as a full-time bookkeeper, is an example.

Once you decide to turn your hobby into a business, you can proceed slowly and cautiously. There is no need to hurry, because you're already earning a living. You can take your time and do it right.

In starting up a business, there is usually a capital investment to make. With a hobby, you already have all or most of the tools and supplies you'll need, and this gives you a flying start.

It gives you flexibility. You don't have to meet a payroll or pay overhead, and therefore can earn money without being forced to have a certain volume of business each month. You can choose the amount of time you want to devote to it, not being confined to a certain schedule.

A fringe benefit of earning money from your hobby, or any underground activity, is the security that comes from having more than one source of income. Most Americans have been indoctrinated to believe that security comes from having a steady job, with a paycheck coming in each week. This is as secure as walking on quicksand, since all your eggs are in one basket, and your economic future can be threatened if you lose that job. Most Americans are aware that perfectly competent workers are laid off every year, through no fault of their own, and that a layoff can hit almost anyone. A company may have to cut back because of a recession, or it may decide to stop producing an unprofitable product, or to buy its subcomponents instead of making them in-house. In each case, employees find themselves out on the street, facing a bleak economic future.

Businessmen know the value of diversification, and you should also be aware that having two or more sources of income gives you additional security, since it is unlikely that all of them will fail you at once.

Almost any hobby can be turned into a money-making venture under the right circumstances. There are two basic types of hobbies — making products and using skills — and they often overlap.

Connie has a skill, painting, which is her hobby. She uses it to turn out products — paintings — that she is able to sell for cash because she has a father-in-law whose business is wholesaling imported picture frames to department stores, and who is able to sell her paintings along with the frames. This gives her a connection which most people don't have. As a housewife, she is able to enjoy her hobby and earn untaxed income by painting in her spare time.

"Red" plays the accordion. He works as a printer during the day, but evenings and weekends he plays his instrument for money. His clientele is of two types: the one-shot who hires him to play at weddings, and his regular accounts, including a social club which books him many Friday and Saturday nights.

Diane is a housewife who likes to write poetry. She has a part-time job teaching literature at a local community college, which earns her some declared income. Like many poets, she went through a long and frustrating period during which she sent her poetry to magazines and accumulated pounds of rejection notices. One day, she decided to take a risk, and had a book of her poetry privately printed. She makes the rounds of the bookstores in her area, selling her books out of the trunk of her car. She sets up a table at art shows, and sometimes sells over a hundred volumes in one day. She reports none of this money.

John, a karate hobbyist, works as a mechanic during the day. On weekends, he holds classes in self-defense, which affords him tax-free income.

Cyril is a stamp collector. He specializes in early American issues, mostly mint, but will not pass up a nicely centered and lightly cancelled used item. He subscribes to stamp magazines, belongs to the local stamp club, and gets the various catalogs, such as Scott's as they come out, in order to monitor prices. He also closely tracks auction results. His knowledge of prices is of great help to him in speculating. When he attends a stamp show, he is easily able to spot undervalued items, and picks them up at bargain prices.

Two days a week, Cyril runs the stamp counter at a local coin shop. He pays the coin dealer $150 a month for his counter. When he is not there, he leaves stamps on display for the coin dealer to sell, and they split the profit from these sales. The coin dealer is happy to have a stamp expert in his shop, since people who stop by to look at stamps often become customers for coins. His deal with Cyril allows him to keep all the money from the sale of stamp supplies. This arrangement gives Cyril a place of business with small overhead and few expenses. All his sales are in cash, and he pays the coin dealer his rent in cash. Cyril has been doing this for six years now, and has never been hassled.

Loretta likes to bake. Her specialty is fruitcakes, laced with brandy and rum, which she sells, at a modest profit, to her friends and neighbors. Each Easter and Christmas, she clears several hundred dollars selling her fruitcakes, which are of much better quality than supermarket and commercial bakery products. Her clients buy her fruitcakes not only for themselves, but as gifts for others. Her main problem is keeping up with the demand, and each season she drafts her husband to help her in the kitchen. Her income is tax-free, of course.

These examples give you an idea of the possibilities for underground entrepreneurship in hobbies. It is a field in which individual intitiative counts for more than in many other money-making ventures. A hobby-business can be as simple or as complicated as you wish to make it. If you decide to use it as a peg for extra deductions, you'll have to get involved in record-keeping, to satisfy the demands of the IRS. If you keep your hobby's earnings completely underground, you can save yourself trouble.

NOTES

1. Internal Revenue Code, Section 183, deals with "Activities Not For Profit," and if you can get through the opaque language, you'll see how the IRS treats those who deduct their hobbies.

16

Traps to Avoid:
Make Money At Home Schemes

If you're interested in earning money on the side, you may have noticed advertisements urging readers to send for details of various methods that promise hundreds of dollars a month in extra income. The ads are aimed at housewives and retirees, and don't give a hint of the difficulties involved.

Some of these are for "pyramid selling" schemes, in which the person starting out is required to buy large stocks of items to sell door-to-door, or by mail. The alleged large volume comes only if you can recruit other people to buy from you and sell the items retail themselves. These schemes are not necessarily frauds in themselves, but the potential for profits is limited.

There are a number which *are* out-and-out frauds,[1] and the Postal Inspection Service has been prosecuting some of them. These usually involve addressing envelopes or manufacturing small items at home. The way they work is to require either a deposit from the victim, or the purchase of supplies with which to run the business. If the scheme requires manufacturing small items, supposedly at a tremendous profit, the company will reject all of the items on the grounds of "defective workmanship," thereby leaving the victim holding the bag. In other schemes, for a fee the victim receives instructions on how to run the business and how to make the product, but he soon finds out that he has to dig up customers on his own, and this proves very difficult indeed.

If you're tempted to answer such an ad, the most important question to ask yourself is: "How come, if this is such a good way of making money, isn't this guy doing it himself instead of sharing his secret with others?" You'll find a common thread running through all these schemes. The ads promise "instant millions" and "sure-fire results," and it is easy to wonder why the advertiser isn't doing it himself and getting richer instead of offering to help others get rich.

Some of the ads are unbelieveable in their tone. One ad shows the president of the company as an altruistic character, who has discovered the basic secret of making big bucks and wants to share it with his fellow suffering humans before departing from this earth, but you must send him a deposit to find out how he does it.

At your local Post Office, you'll find leaflets, put out by the Postal Inspection Service, explaining exactly how these frauds work, and why people who respond to them don't make any money, and lose the deposits they send in. If you see an offer which seems so good to you you're afraid of passing it up, phone the Postal Inspector in your area before mailing off your money. You might be surprised at what he has to say about it, and the price of the phone call will be much less than what you risk losing if the ad is fraudulent.

NOTES

1. *The Rip-Off Book*, by Victor Santoro, Loompanics Unlimited, 1984. This book covers all sorts of frauds and scams, including sections on business opportunity frauds and mail order swindles.

17

Case History:
Don and Shirley's
Underground Used Car Business

Don is a tool and die maker who worked for a small company supplying the auto industry. Ten years ago, he took early retirement. Don and his wife, Shirley, were both 55 years old, and Don had been with the company for over 30 years. They looked forward to traveling and doing the things they had planned for years to do.

The first two years of their retirement were glorious — the pension checks came in on time, Don and Shirley bought a beautiful motor home and spent their winters in Florida. The summers were spent at their Illinois home and visiting their two grown children out west. Everything was rosy.

Then tragedy struck — a tragedy so bizarre and unexpected that to Don and Shirley it was like being hit by lightning. The company Don had worked for went bankrupt, and their pension fund was found to be empty.

Don talked with lawyers and union representatives. Years of litigation followed, and even a U.S. Senator was appealed to on behalf of Don and other retirees, but in the end, nothing could be done. The company's assets were simply *gone*, decimated. After the banks and tax people got their cuts, there was nothing left for Don and the others who had worked so hard for so long.

And that was just the beginning of Don and Shirley's tough luck. Shirley contracted breast cancer, and the treatments were long and expensive. Their medical insurance had come through the bankrupt pension plan, and when the plan went under, their insurance went with it. By this time, they qualified for some help from Medicare, but it was not nearly enough. The difference, and it was a big difference, had to be paid out of their own pockets. Shirley fought and beat the cancer, but the battle exhausted their savings.

Six years after their retirement, things had never looked worse for Don and Shirley. Without their pension, they were unable to travel. Without their savings, they were unprepared for whatever tragedy would strike next. When they first retired, it was fun, because they had enough money to travel and enjoy themselves. But with no pension and no savings, there was little to do except sit around the house and feel sorry for themselves. They had both worked hard for years. They had done everything they were supposed to do. Not only was Don one of the most skilled workers in the plant, but in over 30 years, he had never missed a day — never even been late. No more competent and loyal employee ever worked anywhere, and what did they have to show for it? Don and Shirley had given their lives to the System, and now that it was time for the System to pay them back, all they got was the shaft. They had been Screwed By The System — it was as simple as that.

Even worse than the financial devastation they had suffered was the psychological devastation they now endured. All their lives, Don and Shirley had been cheerful, self-confident people in charge of their fate, and eager to see what life had in store for them each new day. Now Don and Shirley felt like helpless victims, at the mercy of forces beyond their control. They couldn't even find jobs, because they were both "too old." Now they slept later and later each day, and awoke with a feeling of dread, afraid of what new tragedy the day might dump on them. Don and Shirley sure weren't laughing much in those days. With inflation driving up the price of necessities, it was pretty certain they were even going to have to sell their house in order to make ends meet.

And then, in their blackest hour, Don was struck with an odd bit of inspiration — a bit of inspiration that was to mean a whole new lucrative career for him and Shirley, an inspiration that was to give them back their self-esteem, provide them with a good income and financial security, and return the sense of fun and adventure to their lives.

Here is what happened. Don and Shirley had long ago sold their motor home, and now decided to sell their second car, a Pinto several years old, in order to get living expenses for a few months. Shirley put up a notice on the bulletin board at the neighborhood laundromat. They were asking $1,400 for the Pinto, but actually were willing to settle for far less in order to get some quick cash.

Don was surprised at the number of calls they got — within 24 hours, they had received several, and had two people make appointments to look at the car. Don sold the car one morning for $1,200 cash. The other guy had an appointment to look at the car the next afternoon, and when Don called him to notify him that the car had been sold, there was no answer.

Don walked over to the laundromat to take down the "For Sale" notice on the Pinto, and guess what he saw? On the same bulletin board, another person was advertising a Pinto of the same year as Don's! He wanted $1,100. Don stood there looking at that bulletin board. He had $1,200 cash in his pocket. There was a Pinto nearly identical to the one he had just sold which he could buy for $1,100. And there was a guy coming the next afternoon to look at a Pinto Don had advertised for $1,400. If Don could make only $100 out of this situation, that money would be pretty important to him and Shirley.

And thus was born an underground used car dealer.

91

Don quickly took the bus to look at the other car, after calling on the pay phone in the laundromat to make sure it was still for sale. He knocked the guy down to $1,000 by offering him cash on the spot, got a signed title and receipt, and drove the car over to his place. At first, Shirley was puzzled by what Don was doing, but Don just said, "I want to try something here." The second customer showed up the next day, and after a test drive and some dickering, Don sold him the car for $1,250 cash.

Don could hardly wait to get home to tell Shirley what had happened. He had made $250 profit in one day for doing practically nothing! Not only that, but the money was in cash! Don and Shirley talked it over, and they decided to try the same thing again, and it worked just as well the second time. *Now they were in business for keeps.*

That was four years ago, and in those four years, Don and Shirley have made a big success of their underground used car business. Today, they trade 3 or 4 cars a month, averaging $400 profit on each, for just a few hours of "work." And they are paid in untraceable funds, so they pay no taxes on their income. All the money they earn is theirs to keep.

It wasn't easy, though. Don and Shirley worked very hard to learn the right tricks of advertising, buying, selling, and keeping their names out of tax records. Today, Don and Shirley have regained control of their lives. Once again, they can travel — and can even take their used car "business" to Florida or anywhere else they go!

Thanks to the underground economy, these two Guerrilla Capitalists have rebuilt their lives, and once again are productive citizens, instead of being on the edge of welfare.

Here is how they work their business:

Successful buying is the key to any speculative venture, and Don and Shirley have learned many tricks for keeping the buying price down. They purchase cars through many mediums — bulletin boards at colleges, supermarkets, laundromats, etc., from classified ads, and occasionally even from used car dealers. They know *where* they buy is not nearly so important as *what* they buy.

Since they are looking for fast turnover, they select only the most popular cars within any category, since these cars resell faster to less sophisticated buyers. They select mostly smaller cars, like Pintos, Mustangs, etc. These cars appeal to college students and other young people, they have less power equipment for a used-car buyer to worry about, and they are frequently purchased by families as second cars.

Don and Shirley select cars which they can resell for less than $1,500. Most people can pay cash to purchase such a car, whereas they would need to negotiate a loan to buy something more expensive. Don and Shirley are looking for a fast turnover, so any extra time spent by their customer negotiating a loan is money out of *their* pockets. They have found the best thing is to buy no higher than $800-$1,000 so they can resell in the $1,200 to $1,500 range.

They select cars with popular optional equipment. In most cars, they look for an automatic transmission, radio, and heater. Other popular accessories are disk brakes, sunroofs on VW's and power steering on large or medium-sized cars.

When Don and Shirley look through the classifieds, they know which type of cars in which price range and with what accessories to investigate. They especially circle ads which say "best offer" or "must sell" as well as the ones which outright list a low price. When calling, they always maintain they are private parties, while asking about accessories, dents, upholstery, tires and mechanical condition. They know if they say, "We speculate in cars," what they are really saying is, "We are trying to make money off your ignorance," which will not encourage the cooperation of the seller.

Don remembers that he is doing this as a *business,* and time is money, so he doesn't ask useless questions, such as "Have you had much response to your ad?" A question like this gains Don nothing and gives the seller an edge in the bargaining. So Don sticks to the point. A good question to ask is "It's hard for me to get around since I don't have a car — can you bring the car by for me to look at?" Frequently, the seller will bring the car over, saving Don much effort and giving him a psychological advantage in the bargaining session that follows the test drive. In addition, Don finds out if the car isn't registered or doesn't have insurance, and why.

In test-driving the car, Don figures if the engine doesn't smoke, it starts easily, has full power under hard acceleration, and seems to be generally sound, it is okay for his purposes. But when he is in his hardass mode, Don will say he heard a "funny noise" in the engine, or brakes, or whatever. He then takes the car to the appropriate dealer and has the service department suggest the nature of the problem and estimate the cost of repairs. This is his show. With the seller in tow, he stops at muffler shops for muffler questions, brake shops for estimates of how many miles are left on the brakes, and transmission shops for gory stories of how the automatic transmission needs preventive treatment, like a band adjustment, to save it from major repairs only 5,000 miles from now. Don knows he can elicit the most gloomy predictions by stating that he really doesn't know anything about brakes, etc. For example, a good question at the brake shop is, "Why isn't the pedal all the way up?" The answer is *always* "Because you need a brake job" even if the car only needs a pedal adjustment.

Sometimes, out of sympathy for the seller whose time he is consuming, Don tends to get estimates only on "major problems." But he knows that if he is more ruthless, a full show will bring him greater success in the bargaining session because: 1) he has presumably collected reliable estimates of the cost of putting the car into safe driving condition — the seller should be willing to accept a price equal to the average "blue book" value minus these repairs; and 2) Don has convinced him that selling cars is a pain in the ass, making him anxious to unload as quickly as possible and get this unpleasant business over with. Don knows every extra effort he makes is that much more money in his pocket.

In bargaining, Don starts with the average price from one of the "Used Car Prices" guides widely available on newsstands, deducts the cost of repairs, his profit margin, and another $100 or so for horse-trading elbow room, and this is the price he offers for the car.

If the offer is too low for the seller to accept immediately, Don says one of three things:

1. "The price you are asking is for a car in great condition. Considering the quotes for repairs on the muffler, transmission, body work, etc., I would be cheating myself to offer more than (another $50)."

2. "Be realistic. The price you ask may be moderate compared with the other prices in the paper, but everyone knows those prices are intentionally high to make room for horse-trading. Every one of those other cars will sell at a price substantially lower than the price originally asked. My offer, which is a realistic one, is (another $50)."

3. "You may in fact be able to get what you are asking for the car, but my finances are so tight right now that I can only offer (another $50)."

If he haggles to where they agree on a price, Don then leaves a deposit, gets a receipt for the deposit, and makes arrangements to complete the deal. But if the seller is still thinking he can get more for the car, Don doesn't give up. He writes up a little slip of paper (*not* a business card) with his name, phone number, and price he bid, and hands it to the seller, saying something like this: "Here, put this in your wallet so you can contact me if you decide my offer is a fair price for the car." Even if the seller walks away cursing about how Don is trying to steal his great car, Don has found that about one out of three will call him back within a week to accept his offer. (This means Don only has to look at three cars a week to have a tax-free income of $400 per week.)

When the seller calls him back, Don will sometimes say he found out that insurance will be extra expensive so he can only pay $50 less than his previous offer. He knows the seller has tired of the selling process or else he wouldn't have called, and uses this knowledge to get an extra discount. Once in a while, a seller will call to ask Don to increase his offer because he has had a bid equal to Don's from someone else. In a case like this, Don will usually cough up an extra $50, since his original bid included a margin for such dickering.

Since Don is doing this for a living, he keeps accurate records on each car he test-drives, including the seller's phone number and the price he bid. Don has found that if he calls back a week or so after the test-drive, many of the cars will not have been sold, and the seller is much more receptive to his bid.

When he has bought a car, Don must get it ready for market. Some minor repairs will contribute to his ability to resell quickly at a decent profit. Most of the things he does require no mechanical ability or knowledge of engines. They are simple things which will make the car *look* better, and therefore be more saleable. In general, he does all of the things that a used car lot would do to make a car presentable.

He washes the car, and cleans the interior. If the upholstery is torn, Shirley stitches it with upholstery needles and cheap thread from Sears or some other department store. Don washes the engine. To cut thick grease, he uses gasoline applied with a stiff brush or rag, and spruces up the engine compartment with a spray can of black glossy enamel. Don has found that washing the engine is the single most important thing he does to a car. A clean engine in a private party's car says "This car has been babied," or "This is a new engine." Many buyers who say on the phone that they won't buy without getting a complete mechanical check-up will buy on the spot when they see a clean engine. So Don always washes the engine. Don uses Amway clear shoe gloss to make vinyl on dashboards and door panels shine like new, and replaces worn floor mats with carpet remnants from a used carpet store. He removes crystallized acid from battery terminals with a solution of baking soda and water, and replaces bald tires with re-caps. If the paint is dull or pitted with rust, he gets an Earl Scheib paint job for $89.95 in a similar, not necessarily matching, color.

Since Don has acquired a small amount of mechanical ability in his years of dealing with cars, he will also give the car a tune-up and adjust the brake pedal. Before he learned how to do these, he would pay a garage to do them. Don stays away from major repairs. He knows he can sell cars with bad rod bearings and bad clutches just by waiting for the sufficiently naive buyer who always appears when the average popular used car is offered for sale.

In advertising the car for sale, Don has learned the most valuable trick is to let local buyers know it is available; most buyers will look first at a local used car rather than one on the other side of town. He knows his best medium is notices on bulletin boards at colleges, laundromats, supermarkets, etc., for which Don has a carpenter's staple gun. In addition to being the best advertising medium, these places have the advantage of being FREE.

Below is a sample ad for a bulletin board. Don uses the brightest possible paper to make his ads stand out from the many other ads. These ads are especially effective for selling cars to college students. The little "tear-away" phone numbers are a good idea, too, since the person reading it doesn't need to hunt for a pencil and paper to copy down Don's number, and won't remove the entire ad, thereby keeping others from seeing it.

Don always makes his ads more creative than so many which say "excellent condition," and he doesn't use ambiguous phrases like "cherry," "loaded," or meaningless phrases like "cream puff." He doesn't take up valuable space with a lot of crap — he uses it to describe the good features of the car.

In large block letters (a magic marker is good for this), he will say something like "SAVE $300." Then in the typewritten copy, he emphasizes the car's popular features: sunroof, low mileage, new tires, new clutch, or whatever.

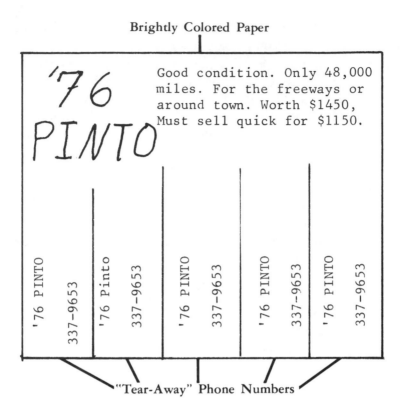

An example of the ads Don and Shirley post around town.

Instead of saying something negative like "dents in body," Don will either say "body fair" or nothing, explaining on the phone that his low price reflects the slight cost of repairing the dents, although the dents can be safely ignored. This way, Don doesn't scare off the handyman who wants to fix it himself or the person who really thinks dents are secondary to mechanical condition.

Don makes his bulletin board ads 5 or 6 to a sheet of paper, and Xeroxes them on colored paper, giving him enough ads to place 2 or 3 on each bulletin board in his vicinity.

Don and Shirley have found their next best advertising medium to be the throw-away classified papers, or "Shopper's Guides," usually given away free at supermarkets, or delivered door-to-door. Not only is advertising cheap in these little papers, but they are well-read, and are good places to sell used cars. In their ads, Don and Shirley use a powerful phrase such as "Super low mileage" or "Super low price," or simply state the mileage, letting the low figure speak for itself.

Here is a sample classified ad:

LOW MILEAGE: '76 Pinto. 48,000 miles. Good condition. Ideal for freeways or around town. Worth $1,450, must sell quick for $1,150. 337-9653.

Another medium Don and Shirley sometimes use is the Sunday classifieds. The same considerations apply as for the Shopper's Guides, discussed above.

In selling the car, Don knows *the most important thing is to appear as a private party, not a dealer.* For reasons of tax avoidance (discussed a little later), Don and Shirley will not have the car in either of their names, so they must have a fabrication in answer to the inevitable question, "Why are you selling?" If the previous owner was male, they can say, "We are selling the car for our grandson, who joined the Air Force. Those dealers who advertise 'cash for your car' wanted to buy it for nothing, so we are helping out our grandson, who is now at training camp." Or he has taken a job out of the country, or they are selling it for Don's brother who has been placed in a rest home, or whatever. If the previous owner was female, they use variations on the same themes: she joined the WACS, or whatever.

In pricing the car, Don always sets the price at least $100 higher than the price he ultimately wants. This allows for horse-trading. Don also sets the price at about the average for the model, or higher, by checking used car dealers' ads in the newpapers. Don has learned that if his price is obviously low, people will think he doesn't have any confidence in the car, and he will get fewer bidders than if he started with a price that is a little high and horse-traded down. Besides, once in a while he gets a buyer who thinks horse-trading is immoral, thereby giving Don an extra $50 or $100 profit. Don sets a floor under his price so that the buyer will start the bidding at a price which guarantees him a profit. This floor also guarantees that he won't be giving test drives to people who lack the money Don needs for his profit.

Now we come to the real *underground* part of Don and Shirley's little business — *avoiding taxes.* The main way Don and Shirley avoid taxes is by remaining invisible to the taxing agencies. *If they don't know you exist, they can't tax you.* Of course, Don and Shirley have no licenses, since such things merely notify the authorities that one is doing business. Essentially, *getting a license is asking to be taxed.* The key to Don and Shirley's whole business is that they pose as private parties, NOT DEALERS, in *all* transactions, and therefore remain invisible, underground entrepreneurs. So Don and Shirley avoid license fees, inventory taxes, business activity taxes, sales taxes, etc., just by simply never telling the tax parasites they are doing business.

It is important that their names not appear in records of ownership, which are processed through the state, and might therefore bring them to attention. They do as follows:

When buying a car, they pay cash, get a receipt, a bill of sale, the properly signed title, and the registration. The key to the transaction is the BILL OF SALE. In speculating, Don and Shirley do not want to have to pay registration expenses on each car they trade, and they want to keep their names off all documents which the government receives so they won't have to buy a dealer's license. *Don and Shirley want it to appear that the car was transferred directly from the previous owner to their customer.* Solutions are:

Method 1: They can forge the previous owner's name onto a bill of sale to be used in the sale of the car to their customer.

Method 2: They can have the previous owner sign a bill of sale which has blank spaces for price, date, and name of purchaser.

Method 3: They can make a Xerox copy of the complete bill of sale with the information pertaining to the sale to their customer on strips of paper pasted over the original information. (They can erase shadow lines off a Xerox copy, or paint around the edges of the original paste-up with 'White-Out," available from office supply stores, before Xeroxing.)

Method 4: They can get a four-leaf carbon speed letter form from their local office supply store, locate the places where the undesireable information will appear, cut holes in the second carbon at the appropriate spots, and complete the original bill of sale on the first sheet — even the most fascist seller will sign without detecting that the third copy will be used to avoid registration expenses.

Method 5: They can simply tell their customer that he doesn't need a bill of sale because, while they will give him a receipt, the government has its own form which he should sign to state on what amount he will have to pay sales tax; or they can say that their bill of sale isn't valid because the only really valid bill of sale is one where he swears before a notary public what price he paid for the car for which he has the signed registration or the signed title.

The best is Method 2. If the seller asks them why they want blank information on the bill of sale, Don and Shirley tell him that the information describing the car, like the serial number, must be on the bill of sale, but they haven't decided for insurance purposes if the car should be registered in one of their names, or in the name of their nephew (or niece, or son-in-law, or whatever). While it won't really hurt anything to fill in the date, Don and Shirley always insist

101

that the price be left blank so they can save some money on sales tax by filling-in a lower sales price later. Most people will understand and not object. If Don and Shirley get a particularly moronic seller, they can always use one of the other methods outlined above.

Below is a sample bill of sale.

BILL OF SALE

Date_____

I, __(previous owner's name)__, hereby sell my 1976 Pinto, color __beige__, serial # _12345678_, for $ _____ cash, to _____.

Signed __(previous owner)_____
Address _____

Witnessed _____
Address _____

Don and Shirley use a Bill of Sale like this one when they buy or sell cars.

This is the format for a bill of sale which can be used to transfer the car directly from the previous owner to Don and Shirley's customer, without them incurring registration expenses. If the transfer of registration is across state lines, or if the title or registration is missing, Don and Shirley get it witnessed by a friend; otherwise, most states don't require a witness. If the previous owner insists on specifying more than the date and car description (even after the arguments Don and Shirley use about why they want the price and purchaser's name left blank), Don and Shirley just let him complete the information, because they can always use one of the other methods above.

102

In selling the car, Don and Shirley remember the ruses they have developed to keep from appearing as dealers in explaining why they are selling a car not registered to them. In selling the car, they accept only cash, cashier's check, certified check, money order, or bank draft. These are all financial instruments which can be easily converted into cash without leaving embarrassing tell-tale stains in bank records.

Don takes the money and hands the buyer: 1) The bill of sale (which he has rigged to transfer ownership directly from the previous owner to the new owner, as described above); 2) The signed title; 3) The registration.

If the buyer wants Don or Shirley to accompany him to get the title transferred, or if he wants a bill of sale stating that they are the agents for the previous owner, Don puts him in his place by offering him a receipt and saying, "Don't be absurd. Can't you see that the title has been signed over by the previous owner? If you want to deduct applicable car expenses from your income tax, I will give you a receipt, but there is nothing else needed to transfer ownership."

Here are a couple of handy little-known facts that Don and Shirley always keep in mind:

1. They don't really even need a title or registration to transfer ownership because these papers may have been lost or the car may have been freshly manufactured from parts. Each state has its own routines, but they all reduce to swearing under oath before a notary that you are the owner. The state then issues a temporary registration while it's checking to be sure the car wasn't stolen. Since Don and Shirley are NOT dealing in stolen cars, they need never have a problem with transferring ownership.

2. The *only* purpose of the bill of sale is to give the state a price on which to charge excise or sales tax. (A car need not be sold in order for it to be necessary to transfer ownership. Cars are frequently transferred from mother to son, brother to brother, or whatever looks plausible without the payment of money, and therefore, with the smallest possible payment of sales tax.)

So now you know all about how Don and Shirley run their little underground used car business. You know how they buy cars, how they sell them, and how they remain "invisible" to the taxing authorities.

And you know the story of how they were shafted by the System, and how they rebuilt their lives in the underground economy. What Don and Shirley are doing is illegal, and they could even go to prison in the unlikely event they are caught. The authorities would call Don and Shirley "cheaters" and "criminals." They would say Don and Shirley are "not paying their fair share." What do *you* think of Don and Shirley? What do *you* think of these honest retirees, who never wanted anything more than to be productive and self-reliant people? *Who* are they "cheating"? *Who* would be better off if they lived in poverty, on welfare, Social Security and food stamps? *Who* would be better off if Don and Shirley still felt like helpless victims, totally dependent on others for their subsistence, dreading the dawn of each new day?

Would *you* be better off if Don and Shirley were forced back onto the dole, either as prison inmates or welfare recipients? Do *you* think Don and Shirley are "criminals"? What kind of System would make these honest, kindly old people into criminals?

Don and Shirley have thought and talked it over, and they have decided that the chance to be self-reliant is worth the risk of apprehension. When it comes to the underground economy, we must each make our own choices. Do you think Don and Shirley made the right choice? If you were in the same situation, what would you have done?

With new car prices so inflated, more and more people are filling their transportation needs with used cars. If you are interested in learning more, there is a 50 page report available which goes into considerable detail as to exactly which cars are best to buy and sell the way Don and Shirley do. It is titled *Underground Car Dealer*, by Maxwell DeSoto, and is available from Underground Reports, 4418 East

Chapman Avenue, Suite 144, Orange, CA 92669. Tell them you read about it in *Guerrilla Capitalism*.

18

Barter

A basic element of the underground economy has existed for about as long as the human race. Money is a recent invention. Trading goods for other goods or for services was the basis of trade for the thousands of years that preceded the invention of money. In turn, buying for cash existed long before checking accounts and credit cards.

Trading goods for other goods is simple, direct, and satisfying. It is also too inefficient to use as a basis for an industrialized economy. Barter requires that the one who needs something and has something to trade for it meet with another person who needs what the first party has to trade and is willing to exchange something that the first party wants.

Money works as a lubricant in transactions. It is a medium of exchange. For centuries, the money system worked well, as it consisted of coins of precious metal, or certificates representing a quantity of precious metal. Today, with inflation and deficit spending, paper currency is debased and even coins are usually not made of precious metal. Add to this the substitution of checks, credit cards and revolving accounts for real money, and a partial return to the barter system is inevitable.

The IRS does not like barter, for the same reason that it does not like cash transactions: they do not leave a paper trail that can be traced and taxed. In fact, one of the first questions that an IRS examiner will ask in an audit is: "Are you a member of a barter exchange?"

One writer has described barter as "a form of individual guerrilla economics, spearheading autonomous attacks on middlemen, taxes, and the corporate squeeze. ...Do not underestimate the power of the swap! It possesses all the advantages of traditional guerrilla tactics. It does not require large troops; it is flexible, hard to pin down, and once it's gone, it leaves no trace. It does not depend on fancy offices, elaborate equipment, or rigid schedules. It works as well in the city as it does in the woods."[1]

Some suggestions have been made for using labor credits as a money substitute, but a quick look will show why this would not work. If people exchanged certificates, each representing an hour of work, inequities would soon appear. A doctor or skilled craftsman would argue that his time is worth more than an unskilled worker, and it would be necessary to assign values to each hour of labor, according to its nature. This would create a paperwork system much like money, and we would be back at our starting point.

Today, barter is mainly useful as a means of avoiding taxes. The IRS's question regarding barter exchanges reveals this.[2] It is necessary to understand exactly how the IRS views barter, and how it enforces its views, to be able to make the best use of barter.

The IRS doesn't tax gifts or small favors.[3] What interests the IRS is goods or services provided that are a person's regular line of work. A plumber who moonlights, or does plumbing work in exchange for goods, will have to be careful not to let the IRS know of this unless he is willing to pay taxes on it. A dentist who extracts a tooth from a mechanic in return for a tune-up is liable to a tax bite, if the IRS finds out. A person who lends his lawnmower to a neighbor in exchange for the loan of a spray gun is in another category, as these are personal favors and not taxable.

The key phrase is: "If the IRS finds out." With no money changing hands, and no paperwork trail, it is hard for the IRS to find out.

Despite the money system, barter is common among businesses. The term used is "trade-out." A hotel chain, for example, will trade out accommodations in return for advertising. In such cases, the nature and amount of the trade-out has to show on the tax return, and is treated as income according to its "fair market value," which means value as if it had been sold. Large companies, because of their intricacies and detailed bookkeeping, cannot easily hide trade-outs, and usually pay taxes on them. Still, they find trade-outs profitable, as they can enter them at a discounted value. Discounts are common in many businesses, and in this application are useful as tax saving measures.

While barter of personal items and services is common among individuals and not taxable anyway, such barter among businessmen often takes place "off the books."

Vince, a photographer, took photographs for a restaurant owner. Informally, without stipulating that this was payment, the restaurateur invited him to a choice meal. He also gave him some steaks to take home with him. Later, during an assignment in a motel, he provided some extra prints for the manager. The manager invited Vince and his wife to spend a night in the motel's new waterbed suite. Neither of these two nor many similar transactions ever found their way onto Vince's tax return.

Barter is not just a device used by unskilled or illiterate individuals who have little to trade. It is often used by those who already have high incomes and profitable skills to avoid paying more than what they feel is their fair share of taxes. Doctors, lawyers and other professionals use barter.

Ross, a computer specialist and woodworking hobbyist, earns an income far above average, and consequently pays more than the average amount in taxes. He systematically uses barter, exchanging his skills and products for goods and services. His wife's last baby was delivered by a midwife who took a playhouse for her daughters in exchange. As Ross is a skilled woodworker, the playhouse, measuring eight feet square, was a work of art.

Ross also refinished an antique table in exchange for a painting by an acquaintance who is an artist. The artist is currently doing another painting for Ross, who is making a tea cart for him.

Ross acquired an air compressor and spray gun, for which he traded a hand-made trestle table and benches. Ross's family doctor provides medical services at no charge, while Ross reciprocates by making him a magazine rack and other office furniture.

In his line of work, Ross has "bought time" on computers in exchange for designing programs for their owners. His family barters actively, too. His oldest daughter trades babysitting for concert tickets.

We see from this quick sketch of Ross's bartering that it takes in the spectrum from an exchange of personal favors, which is not normally taxable, to outright trade of professional services, which is. In this one instance we can see the many reasons why the IRS is so concerned about bartering. Not only is it hard to trace, and thereby hard to tax, but in many instances it falls into a legal gray area. Where there is an unmistakable trade of professional services, there is no question. However, in the case of the family doctor, the doctor is trading his services, while Ross is giving him wood furniture, and woodworking is Ross's hobby, not his trade. Linda, Ross's daughter, is a minor. While theoretically income from babysitting is taxable, it is hard to imagine even the IRS auditing a minor.

The major problem in barter is meeting people who want to trade with you, and have something you want. You might be tempted to join a barter club, as many have recently. This will expose you to a risk, unless you are prepared to pay taxes on your trades. Barter exchanges, by their very nature, have to keep records. Right now, there is no law requiring them to send periodic reports to the IRS, but this could change suddenly. Even now, in individual cases, the IRS can subpoena their records, and one proprietor of such an exchange warns that this could happen.[4] Therefore, if you want to be a successful Guerrilla Capitalist, stay away from barter exchanges.

NOTES

1. *The Barter Book*, Dyanne Asimow Simon, Doubleday, 1979.
2. *Fundamentals of Successful Bartering,* Ron Levy, Koala Press, Santa Barbara, 1982, p. 36.
3. *Ibid.,* p. 38.
4. *Inside the Underground Economy,* Jerome Tuccille, New American Library, New York, 1982, p. 83.

19

Starting Out In Bartering

We've seen how barter is useful for evading taxes. There is also another use for barter: survival. This is a little-understood and emotional topic, often sensationalized for the sake of selling books and magazines. In reality, "survival" simply means coping with many threats. Some are threats to your life, such as riots and nuclear war. Other more common threats are threats to your lifestyle, such as taxes, inflation and gas shortages. Trading goods and services instead of paying cash is one way of coping.

To prepare for bartering, assess your skills and possessions. What do you have to trade? People need both products and services. Your products and skills can be either something you do as an occupation, or as a hobby or second trade. *Some products you could use for barter are:*
- Foods grown in your back yard.
- Things you can make, such as furniture or sculptures.

Some services you can use for barter are:
- Babysitting, which does not require great skill.
- Plumbing and electrical contracting.
- Midwifery.
- Tutoring.
- Medical care.

- Accounting or bookkeeping.
- Manual labor of various sorts, such as helping with a harvest in return for food.

We have seen that the central problem with bartering is that the two parties must meet face to face and have items that each wants. We have also seen that one way to compensate for this inefficiency is a barter exchange, which exposes the participants to the risks of dealing with the IRS. There is another way. In ancient societies, people soon found items that were useful as media of exchange, such as salt. The old expression, "not worth his salt," came from this practice.

A medium of exchange works like money. It is a commodity everyone can use, is durable, and is commonly accepted as having value. We can call it *barter currency.*

Barter currency is different from fiat currency, or money, in at least one significant way: it has value by itself, unlike money. You can't eat money. You can't build a house with it. You can paper your walls with Federal Reserve notes, and you can use coins for slingshot ammunition, neither of which is very practical. Barter currency has immediate and practical value. Salt, one of the oldest, is obviously and commonly useful. In our industrialized society, other items have value as barter currency, such as .22 ammunition[1] and fuel.

Fiat currency, or money, has value because the government says it does. Money used to be backed by commodities of commonly accepted value, but no longer. Now it is just the product of a printing press, and this debased currency is directly linked to inflation.[2]

Thus, we see you can work barter two ways: by a direct swap of your skill or product for something you need, or by exchanging it for something you can use as "trade goods" later — or barter currency.

You can get a head start in barter currency by buying some for cash now, while it is still commonly available at a low

114

price. Buying commodities is one way of making your savings inflation-proof[3] and preparing for possible shortages or even a breakdown of the economy.

Some items are better than others as choices for barter currency, for various reasons. Above all, barter currency must store well, which limits the possibilites. Secondly, it must be commonly accepted. Let's look at a few obvious prospects:

Canned and Dried Foods. These are obvious, as people always need to eat. The limitation is that foods do not keep as well as some other, more durable items.

Alcoholic Beverages. These have always been in demand, and probably always will be. They keep well, as a rule, although some not as well as others.[4]

Silver Coins. Although you definitely can't eat silver, a lot of people will accept coins made of this metal as having real value. This is a critical point. Real value partly depends on the opinions and perceptions of the person making the judgment, and a commodity that is accepted by a great many people is useful, even though the person using it may not have any need for it himself. The next item is an excellent example of this principle.

Cigarettes. We know that smoking is harmful, and many people do not smoke because their religion forbids it. Yet, in the 20th Century, cigarettes have been widely used as barter currency, such as in post-war Germany, and are worth stockpiling for this reason.

Ammunition. This is a gun-oriented society, but apart from that, hunting with firearms is one common way of getting food. The most widely-used caliber of gun is the .22 Long Rifle which, despite the name, is used in both rifles and pistols. .22 ammo is compact, not very expensive, and keeps well. It is important to note that some brands keep better than others, and if you're thinking of stockpiling ammunition, it is worthwhile to run a test to find out which store best. Take a box of each brand you want to test, open it, and leave it outside, in your yard or on the roof, for a few weeks, where it will be exposed to the elements. Then test-fire it. You will see there will be more misfires with some brands than others, and this will give you an idea of what brands store best in your locale.

Primers. Many gun hobbyists reload their shells, and a fresh primer is essential for each reloaded cartridge. While it is possible to improvise the manufacture of gunpowder, primers are much more difficult to make. Right now, they are cheap, and they are compact and easy to store. In some locales, where there are a lot of reloaders, primers will be an excellent medium of exchange.

This is a very incomplete list, and you might find many other items worth stockpiling as barter currency, such as fuel, motor oil, batteries, and even medicines. The choice is up to you, and one important factor is whether or not you are in a position to buy some of these items cheaply. If, for example, you have a friend who owns a gun store, you may be able to persuade him to sell you cartridges and primers wholesale. If you're a pharmacist, you can stockpile medicines. If you work in a food business, you may be able to get various food products at a good price, stretching your limited dollars further.

To start out in barter, it is important to develop a barter mentality. While it is difficult to walk into a store and offer barter instead of cash, in some instances you can work out trades with friends and neighbors. If some of them own small businesses, you may be able to work trades for items they make or handle.

Right now, while the currency is still relatively stable, you can build up a list of traders. You can help spread the practice by encouraging others to barter instead of paying cash.

If you live in a rural area, you're probably already bartering, as barter is an established practice among farmers.[5] In a city, it is not as common, and you may be tempted to join a barter exchange.[6] Don't do it, for reasons you already know.

116

Barter is one key to survival. It will help you in the short run to survive the ravages of taxation, and in the long run you'll have a means to cope if the economy crashes, whether it is a sudden crash or a long downward slide, as we are seeing now.

NOTES

This is an extensive and fascinating subject. There are many sources available, each with a somewhat different point of view. Some of them are, as cited in the chapter:

1. *Survival Bartering,* Duncan Long, Long Survival Publications, PO Box 163, Wamego, KS 66547, 1981. Page 18 discusses stockpiling both .22 ammunition and silver coins, and some of the ins and outs connected with this.

2. *The Alpha Strategy,* John A. Pugsley, Stratford Press, Los Angeles, 1981. Part one of this book discusses how what we accept as money has been, and is still being, debased, so those who deal in it are constantly being hurt by inflation, which actually destroys more of the value of an individual's efforts than does taxation. While the discussion seems simplistic in spots, it is fundamentally correct, and will give the reader a crash course in survival economics.

3. *The Alpha Strategy,* pages 153-188 include discussion of how investing in real goods will prevent being hurt by inflation much more than other forms of investment.

4. *The Alpha Strategy,* pp. 167-171. There are ins and outs to stockpiling wines and other alcoholic beverages, and these pages give an introduction to the fundamentals.

5. *Let's Try Barter,* Charles Morrow Wilson, Devin-Adair, 1976. This is a sampling of how barter works in rural societies, as well as some suggestions for its use in the 20th Century.

6. *The Barter Way to Beat Inflation,* George W. Burt, Everest House, New York, 1980. This book covers many of

the everyday details of barter, but unfortunately is oriented toward barter clubs and exchanges, which we have seen are traps for the naive. Still, there is useful information in this volume.

Yet another book, short and easy to read, is *Fundamentals of Successful Bartering,* by Ron Levy, Koala Press, Santa Barbara, CA, 1982. This deals in a concise way with determining values, negotiating, and closing the deals. Unfortunately, the author pushes barter clubs, and you'll do well to ignore that advice.

The value of barter and other guerrilla methods is recognized in a "mainstream" book on finance, *Strategic Investing,* by Douglas Casey, Simon and Schuster, 1982. His chapter on what he calls the "alternative economy," pp. 158-166, deals with what we have been discussing in this book, and Casey recommends underground methods to assure survival in an era of increasing inflation and taxation. You can be sure the IRS doesn't like this book.

20

Deal In Cash!

One of the recently started myths of the 20th Century is that of the "cashless society." This view, laid out in many magazine articles over the past decade, proposes that, with the widespread use of computers and credit cards, nobody will use cash anymore in the near future. The paycheck will go into the employee's account, and he will pay for all his purchases with an electronic card, with the amount instantly deducted from his account by means of a computer linkage.

This system has many benefits, according to the mythmakers: There will be no need for cash, making robbery obsolete. The computer will make bad checks impossible, as it will provide an instant survey of the payer's account to determine whether or not there are enough funds to cover the purchase. The individual's bookkeeping will be done for him, by computer, making the filling out of tax forms easy.

There are several things wrong with this idea:

1. It will make government surveillance of any person's finances easy — a necessary prerequisite for total taxation. With computerized records, the IRS will be able to trace nearly every cent earned and every cent spent by nearly everyone in the country.

2. Such a plan, if implemented, would knock the bottom out of a lot of the underground economy, which is probably the main idea behind such an expensive and far-reaching step.

3. It simply doesn't work. The people aren't buying it. Proof of this is given in a study by Professor Peter Gutman, in the *Financial Analysts Journal*, Nov./Dec. 1977, in which he states there is a large amount of cash circulating, despite the growth of the checking and credit card industries. In a statement to Congress,[1] Gutman said in 1976, that there was $480 in cash circulating for each person in the United States. He added that we are not becoming a "cashless society," but using *more* cash.

The IRS confirms this, stating that on April 1, 1979, there were $100 billions of dollars in general circulation.[2]

From this, it is obvious that not only is there a huge underground economy in this country, but that, logically, the people involved deal mainly in cash.

The reasons are obvious. Cash is basically untraceable. A check must be redeemed, and this leaves a record in at least two places: the payer's checking account, and the records of the person who cashes or deposits the check.

Bank records, while supposedly private, can easily be subpoenaed by the IRS. They provide documentation to an IRS investigator who is trying to establish unreported income.

Cash is the way to go for the Guerrilla Capitalist. The IRS proves this in their report dealing with unreported income,[3] where they show that those who gain income through salaries, involving W-2 forms, are able to understate their incomes far less than those who are self-employed and deal in cash.

The lesson is clear. The Guerrilla Capitalist can "forget" to report income in cash, but should include on his tax return income which he receives in checks, as they are traceable if the IRS starts digging.

If the Guerrilla Capitalist does get paid with a check, there are a couple of things he can do to minimize traces in his own bank records. Rather than depositing the check in his own bank account, the Guerrilla Capitalist will endorse the check to someone else and use it to pay a bill of his own. For example, Tom the underground trucker gets a check from a contractor for cleaning up a building site. Instead of depositing the check, Tom endorses it over to a garage and uses it to buy gas and oil for his truck and van.

Another thing a Guerrilla Capitalist can do with a check is take it to the bank it was drawn on and cash it right there. This keeps it out of the undergrounder's bank records.

NOTES

1. *Hearings Before the Joint Economic Committee, Congress of the United States, Ninety-Sixth Congress, First Session*, Nov. 15, 1979, U.S. Government Printing Office, Wash. D.C., p. 29.

2. *Estimates of Income Unreported on Individual Tax Returns*, Dept. of the Treasury, Internal Revenue Service, Publication 1104(9-79), p. 30.

3. *Ibid.*, pp. 6-9.

21

The Trouble With Banks

Banks are one possible place to put unreported income, and many people do it, but the practice is dangerous.

Years ago, it was possible to open a bank account under an assumed name. There was no requirement for I.D., and a slush fund could be stashed openly in a savings account, collecting interest, for years. Today, with the new law requiring withholding of a portion of the interest earned, most banks ask for not only a Social Security number, but formal I.D. when a new customer opens an account.

The reason some people are able to get away with stashing unreported income in a bank account is that the IRS audits so few returns, and carries out major investigations of even fewer yet. The fact that so many get away with it can lead to a feeling of complacency, and this can be dangerous for the serious Guerrilla Capitalist.

With the proliferation of computers, bank records are increasingly available to the IRS. Now, the IRS has access to the information regarding the interest you earned. From this, it can infer your income level, and, more importantly, compare your figures with the averages. Anyone showing above-average bank balances will run the risk of special attention, just as anyone who exceeds the norms for certain deductions is singled out.

Recognizing that banks generally require I.D. of their new customers, some undergrounders choose to use false I.D. Banks require not only a Social Security number, but a driver's license, passport, or other form of official I.D., preferably with a photograph of the owner. For the person who has to live completely underground, false I.D. is part of his lifestyle. For the person who is moonlighting, but otherwise above ground, false I.D. may be too much trouble.[1] While the undergrounder may accept the fact that a certain portion of his interest income will be withheld, the paper trail that a bank account leaves in regard to his other income may be unacceptable.

There are other ways to use banks as hiding places for undeclared income. The most obvious is the safe deposit box. This is a trap, however, and many people fall into it. The law permits the fee for rental of a safe deposit box to be deducted, and many do. The purpose behind this piddling allowance is obvious. Anyone who claims such a deduction tells the IRS that he has a safe deposit box,[2] and this is one of the first things the IRS looks for in an investigation.

So undergrounders in the know avoid having safe deposit boxes in banks, although some do rent them in assumed names, using false I.D.

Some banks have non-interest-bearing accounts available to their depositors. The most common form is a checking account. Since there is no interest paid, the bank does not send a Form 1099 to the IRS, but it still requires I.D. The reason for this is "recourse," a term which means the bank must know whom to contact to make good on a check. The problem of bad checks is serious, and banks want to know with whom they are dealing to protect themselves.

A non-interest-bearing account is slightly less dangerous for the Guerrilla Capitalist than one which pays interest, in that the bank does not automatically advertise the account's existence to the IRS — but in an investigation, it may be forced to reveal it.

Another problem with banks is that they are required by the government to keep microfilmed records of every check you write and also every check you deposit. A little thought will reveal just how easily a person's financial transactions for any period can be reconstructed with this information.

From the discussion in this chapter, it is evident that the wise Guerrilla Capitalist will use banks as little as possible for his unreported dealings.

NOTES

1. Some excellent books which detail the procedures for obtaining fake I.D. are: *The Paper Trip I & II*, Eden Press, PO Box 8410, Fountain Valley, CA 92708. *New I.D. In America*, by Anonymous, Paladin Press, PO Box 1307, Boulder, CO 80306. *How to Get I.D. in Canada and Other Countries*, by Ronald George Eriksen 2, Loompanics Unlimited, PO Box 1197, Port Townsend, WA 98368. *I.D. For Sale*, by Michael Hoy, Loompanics Unlimited.

2. *How to Cheat On Your Taxes*, by "X," C.P.A., 1040 Press, 1982, p. 77.

22

How Small Businessmen Fiddle the Books

Mr. Joe Wage-Earner gets it in the neck: his income tax is taken out of his pay before he even receives it! Not much chance to do any "fiddling" there.

Having one's own business, on the other hand, opens up a lot of opportunities for creative accounting. Since the small businessman reports *his own* income, he can greatly reduce his tax liability by "adjusting" financial figures.

Skimming is one such opportunity. Skimming simply means taking cash off the top of the receipts and not reporting this money as income. Nearly any retail business receiving a decent proportion of its receipts in cash can do this. If you took in $200 today, take $25 and put it in your pocket. Report $175 as receipts on your taxes. It's as simple as that. Audit trails have to be watched out for, though. If the businessman reports his sales from his cash register tapes, he will just simply leave the cash drawer open and not ring up any sales for the last couple hours or so of the day.

Skimming is best kept within reasonable bounds. It is best done by taking just a little, say 10%-20%, off the top, and still deducting all expenses. If you start skimming more than that, you are going to encounter a problem. The profit margin on your business will be lower than "normal," and this is one thing an income tax auditor looks for. What some do to get around this is hide expenses as well as income. They literally keep two sets of books.

Suppose a guy is skimming 50% off the top of his receipts. He knows that if he deducts all his expenses, his tax return will appear very abnormal. So, he also hides half of his expenses. He does this by paying these expenses in cash, so no record is left in his bank account, and then just throwing those receipts away. In this case, he is actually conducting half of his business off the books. This can get pretty tricky, but is quite widely done.[1]

It is the opinion of this author that a person is better off hiding only receipts, instead of both receipts and expenses, but each Guerrilla Capitalist must weigh the consequences and then choose his or her own tactics.

Other ways of taking cash out of a business. Even if the Guerrilla Capitalist is paid with a check or money order, he can still avoid reporting the income on his taxes, in a couple of ways. The check or money order can simply be taken to the bank it is drawn on and endorsed and cashed right there. Postal money orders can be cashed at the post office. Or he can endorse checks or money orders and use them to pay bills — a "second party check."

Another thing that can be done is for the Guerrilla Capitalist to deposit all the checks in his bank, but get cash back when he makes the deposit. He fills out the deposit slip, listing all the checks, and then at the bottom, requests a cash withdrawal directly on the deposit slip. Some deposit slips even have a place especially for this purpose — see example on next page.

This way, a smaller amount is deposited, and it is the net amount of the deposit that appears on the Guerrilla Capitalist's bank statement. This is risky, in that if the IRS was really out to get a guy, they could subpoena the bank's copies of all one's deposit slips, but they seldom ever do that. On nearly every audit, the normal IRS procedure is to add up

		CASH	$	
████████ SERVICES		C H E C K S		
P O BOX ████				
HADLOCK, WA 98339				
DATE: *Sept. 26, 1984*		TOTAL FROM THE REVERSE SIDE	1285	67
All items are received for purposes of collection. All credits for items are provisional until collected.		SUB TOTAL		
CASH RECEIVED BY: *Adam Cash*		LESS CASH (−)	400	00
		TOTAL DEPOSIT	885	67

PA **Port Angeles**
savings & loan association
215 TAYLOR STREET
PORT TOWNSEND, WASHINGTON 98368

⑈3251708511⑈0 ████████████

Bank Check Supply

DEPOSIT

*The deposit slip above shows how you can slip-up the tax auditors by
making a cash deduction before the deposit enters your account.*

the deposits from your bank statements and then compare
the total with the income you reported on your income tax
return.

This is a good place to talk about consistency in your tax
returns. If any of your business at all is on the books, you will
be filing several different tax returns. The wise Guerrilla
Capitalist will make sure that all these returns reconcile with
each other, since it is a common audit practice to examine
returns other than the one being audited, to make sure that
income and expenses are consistent. For example, if you
deduct, $XXX.xx for "labor expense," you better make sure
that your figures for "labor" are the same on all your tax
returns. The figure for labor on your income tax return
should be exactly the same as the amount on your state
unemployment tax return, your state income tax return, your
form for paying state withholding, your workmans'
compensation return, etc. Likewise with your receipts: the

129

amount reported on your income tax return should be exactly the same as the amount on your state sales tax return, etc. And so on down the line. A set of books that is internally consistent with itself has a much better chance of getting through an audit than a set riddled with contradictions.

Now let's look at some ways of fiddling those tax returns.

Inventory adjustments. Due to the way "income" is figured for purposes of federal income tax, small businessmen are forced to pay taxes on their inventory. Stock on hand at the year end is considered an asset of the business, and money spent on this inventory is not deductible until the stock is sold. Thus, the small businessman spends his income on inventory, and still has to pay taxes on that money, even though he hasn't sold the stock yet. The lower the inventory at the end of the year, the smaller the tax liability. Businessmen are supposed to perform an actual physical count of their inventory at the end of the tax year, but some "estimate." As long as the "adjustment" is kept within reason, the chances of being caught are almost non-existent. For example, a well-stocked convenience store may have $90,000 in inventory — or maybe it is only $75,000, instead. By the time an auditor appears on the scene, how could he tell the difference?[2]

"Extra" cash paid-outs. Here is an easy one that can add up over a period of time. Most supermarkets and many other stores now have cash registers that print on the register tape exactly what it is you bought, so this one won't work with receipts from those stores. But say you go in the local mom and pop grocery and buy a six pack of beer, a package of cheese, and a Sunday paper. The receipt they give you will have only the prices and total listed, with no indication of what it was you bought. So the Guerrilla Capitalist will put this receipt in his business paid-outs, after first scribbling "ballpoint pens, tape, and stamp pad," or something similar, on it. He then deducts this as an office expense on his income tax. Some Guerrilla Capitalists have even been known to purchase receipt books and pads of invoices at the

130

office supply stores, and fill them in with "cash paid-outs."
Every little bit helps.

Recording personal expenses as business expenses. This is
very similar to the one above. Let's say the Guerrilla
Capitalist goes to the supermarket and buys a bunch of
window cleaner, toilet paper, hand soap, vacuum cleaner
bags, etc., for his house. The supermarket receipt will list
these items, but it doesn't say the guy is taking them home.
How will an auditor know this stuff wasn't used at the
office? This can also be done with magazine subscriptions,
stereo equipment (music system for your office), building
supplies, camera equipment, etc., etc. Even meals in
restaurants can be deductible, if they were "business" meals.

We have covered here only a few of the more likely ways a
Guerrilla Capitalist can fiddle his books. In practice, what
you can do is limited mainly by your imagination and
willingness to take risks. One entire book has been written
on the subject, and is must reading for all Guerrilla
Capitalists.[3]

NOTES

1. *The Mirage,* by Smith and Zekman, Random House,
1979. This book has an excellent chapter on skimming.

2. *How to Cheat On Your Taxes,* by "X," C.P.A., 1040 Press,
1983. This book contains an excellent section on inventory
adjustments.

3. *Ibid.*

23

What Guerrilla Capitalists Do With Their Unreported Income

For most of us, this is not a severe problem — we spend it as soon as we get it, just to make ends meet. However, some Guerrilla Capitalists, while not getting filthy rich overnight, will have enough of a surplus to inspire them to seek ways of using the extra income that will not bring them to the attention of the IRS.

We have seen that the key to staying out of the clutches of the tax man is to keep a low profile. Keeping your purchases inconspicuous and not leaving a paperwork trail is vital to this end. Charging an expensive vacation to Bermuda on your credit card is a very good way to leave a paper trail that will be difficult to explain away if you are ever audited.

If you decide to buy consumer goods, such as furniture or a stereo system, buy for cash and don't keep the receipts. That way, you can always claim you bought the articles cheaply at a garage sale or a second-hand store.

Some people, not having enough immediate needs to absorb the extra income, will want to find some way of saving it. We already know that putting it into a bank is the kiss of death, because of the paperwork involved. We have seen banks are required to make reports on accounts, and this could tip off the IRS. But what about safe deposit boxes?

Is it safe to keep that extra cash in a safe deposit box in a bank? No it isn't. In fact, this is one of the most dangerous mistakes a Guerrilla Capitalist can make.

The reason for this is that if a tax auditor knows you have a safe deposit box, he can guess at what you have in there, without having to look himself, and without you even knowing you are under investigation! While a taxman would need a subpoena to actually get into your safe deposit box, he needs no subpoena to look at the records of *when* you got into the box. Tax investigators are trained to reconstruct your financial history from just such scraps of information as this. For example, if an auditor learns that you visit your safe deposit box every Monday, he would suspect that you were doing something to generate income on the weekends, which means he is tipped off to the fact that you are a Guerrilla Capitalist.[1] The wise Guerrilla Capitalist will avoid not only bank accounts, but safe deposit boxes in banks as well.

In any event, saving cash, in most forms, means watching your precious savings shrink from inflation. For the hard-core Guerrilla Capitalist, real goods are the only things that are inflation-proof.

Buying and stockpiling items that you know you'll be using sooner or later is a splendid way of both disposing of your extra income and of beating inflation.[2] It is important enough to rate mention in a "mainstream" book on investing.[3] We can categorize this as "survival stockpiling." It is a cushion against hard times, loss of income, collapse of the economy, and all of the other threats to your lifestyle that are happening now and may happen in the future.

Putting money into fixing up one's own home is a good way to spend/invest unreported money. Many Guerrilla Capitalists remodel their homes with things like nice cedar paneling they have bought for cash at lumber yards in neighboring towns. The wise undergrounder avoids building permits.

Unreported money can also be reinvested in the underground business, itself. Acquiring better tools and equipment, and stockpiling supplies can soak up some of that untaxed income.

Some may be interested in investments. The problem here is that most forms of investment are traceable, which puts you in the uncomfortable position of having to explain where you got the money to invest. Another more serious drawback, even for the above-ground investor, is that most of the conventional forms of investment are volatile and uncertain. The stock market is the most conspicuous example. Every year, we see a flood of books on the stock market come out, each with its "system" of beating the market and getting rich quickly. The obvious question that comes up is: "Why is the author not taking his own advice and getting rich by playing the market, instead of wasting his time writing a book and telling everyone his secrets?"

The hard, brutal fact is that getting rich in the market is mainly a matter of luck, and there is no reliable way of predicting the future in stocks. This is explained very well in a current book.[4] Anyone who invests in stocks, bonds, or futures is gambling, and he stands to lose his investment.

Another hard fact about playing the market is that you have to work through a broker, who collects his commission on every transaction. His cut, taken off the top, eats into any profit you might make, and you have to pay his commission even if you take a loss.

Some of the more prudent investors choose to place their funds in investments that are untraceable, durable, and easy to store secretly. One excellent example is silver coins, which have steadily increased in value since the government stopped minting them. Despite large fluctuations in the market value of silver in the last decade, coins have retained their value, and today no silver coin is worth less than its face value.

Silver coins are easy to buy without paperwork. Although some brokers handle them, it is also possible to buy silver coins in coin shops for cash, and from private individuals.

Coins do not deteriorate with age, and are liquid, which means they are easily spent, at any time, anywhere. By contrast, ingots of precious metal are not as liquid. You can't buy a tank of gasoline with a bar of silver, gold, or platinum. To get your profit, you have to sell it through a broker most of the time, and that exposes you at least to a capital gains tax, if not further investigation by the IRS.

Which brings us to what to do with the investments you are holding. One easy answer is to bury them or hide them in some other way. There are many ways to construct hiding places in your home, both to evade search by the IRS or, more likely, as protection against burglary.[5,6]

Open stockpiling is another answer. Many families normally keep a supply of canned food on hand, and many people who own cars keep spare parts, such as points, plugs and tires. This is so common that it attracts little attention from either neighbors or the IRS, and is a good way to lay something aside for the future.

Some people feel that underground income is "mad money" to be used for purposes that would otherwise be impractical. Expensive hobbies are one way to spend hidden income, as long as the hobby is not conspicuous. If your hobby is cars, having a Rolls-Royce parked in your driveway will make you stand out, may inspire a jealous neighbor to report you to the IRS, and may be a sign to criminals that you are worth kidnapping or robbing.

Some people like nightclubbing, and those who do know it is easy to spend several hundred dollars in an evening. This is an untraceable way of spending untraceable income. Another way is gambling, for those who have the fever. A trip to Las Vegas or Atlantic City is easy to disguise, if you tell your neighbors that you're going to visit your Aunt Minnie in Podunk, and pay for everything in cash.

Travel is yet another way to spend hidden income on yourself, as long as you don't visit any country that requires a passport, which would betray your trips. We are fortunate to live in the United States, with its large area, and to have neighboring countries which do not require passports to visit. If you want to keep the scale and expense of your travel hidden, don't send back picture postcards from Maine or Vancouver, as the case may be.

Eating out is another practical way to spend money without leaving a trail, and it is a good way if you enjoy eating but hate to cook or brownbag. Brownbagging your lunch is an excellent way to save money, and the reverse is quite true. While you can spend as little as two or three dollars a week by having Granola bars for lunch, if you like elegant dining, you can easily spend fifty. Taking the wife out to dinner several times a week can get rid of between twenty and fifty or more dollars a throw, and if you remember to pay cash and not run your mouth off to friends, it is truly untraceable.

Most forms of entertainment, while they may seem unduly self-indulgent to some, are ways of spending hidden income in an inconspicuous way, and this appeals to some people who like to live the high life.

Whatever your lifestyle, whether you choose to invest for the future or spend it now, there are ways to dispose of your bonus income without attracting attention to yourself. The basic rule is to keep a low profile. Just use common good sense. Don't go driving around in a Jaguar wearing $600 suits when you are reporting $6,500 a year on your income tax return. Treating your new wealth wisely is as important as earning it.

NOTES

1. *Advanced Investigative Techniques for Private Financial Records*, Richard A. Nossen, Loompanics Unlimited, 1984. The author was a criminal investigator for the IRS for 24 years, and in this book he reveals how the IRS determines unreported income,' undisclosed financial interests, etc.

Written for government investigators, this is a manual on how to catch people for income tax invasion, and should be read carefully by every Guerrilla Capitalist.

2. *The Alpha Strategy*, John A. Pugsley, Stratford Press, Los Angeles, 1981. Pages 147-210 lay out a strategy of investment that is applicable to anyone who has even a slight surplus income, and who is interested in safe ways of providing for the future.

3. *Strategic Investing*, Douglas Casey, Simon and Schuster, 1982. Pages 177-188 deal with stockpiling, or hoarding, and offer good advice on what to stockpile and how to do it.

4. *The Alpha Strategy*, pp. 100-130, explain in detail the problems associated with playing the market, and why predicting the future prices of stocks is such a risky undertaking.

5. *How to Hide Anything*, by Michael Connor, Paladin Press, 1984. An excellent book on constructing secret hiding places inside and outside of the home.

6. *How to Bury Your Goods*, by Eddie the Wire, Loompanics Unlimited, 1981. This is the most comprehensive manual ever written on methods of long-term underground storage. For the hardcore individualist who does not trust banks, governments, social planners, or anyone else.

24

The Face of The Enemy:
A Quick Look at The I.R.S.

The I.R.S. is a bureaucratic monster that, from a very modest start, has grown and grown. In 1914, a person with $20,000 in taxable income was taxed at 1%, someone with $500,000 in taxable income was liable for a whopping 7%. In 1914, the income tax paid per capita was 28 cents; today it is $1,217.77. In 1914, the IRS had 4,200 employees; today it has 82,857.[1]

As with any bureaucracy that has gotten out of control, its rules and procedures are arbitrary and unfair. For example, in the area of deductions, you can deduct the cost of doctor's fees, but you cannot deduct the price of a health spa to help keep you in shape. If you sell your house at a profit, that profit is taxable unless you buy another house within a specific period. However, if you sell it at a loss, you cannot deduct the loss at all. Birth control pills are deductible, but not maternity clothes. A working man who goes out to lunch with his shop buddies cannot write it off, but a "businessman" who takes his "business associates" to a "business lunch" can. Toothbrushes and toothpaste, to keep your teeth healthy, are not deductible, but if you get a cavity, the cost of a dentist is.

Every now and then the government has a tax reduction. In 1965, the basic rate went down from 20% to 14%, while in the top bracket, the rate dropped from 95% to 70%. Recently, the rate for the top incomes dropped from 70% to 50%, a full 20 point reduction. If the IRS were consistent, the 20% bracket people should now be tax-free, but we know they are not.

Many middle class people feel the major part of the tax burden is on their shoulders, and unfortunately, the facts bear them out. Those on welfare, with no income, obviously pay no taxes, and the wealthy can afford to hire high-priced lawyers and accountants to find the tax loopholes that often result in their paying a ridiculously low amount of tax on an enviably high income.

For years, the number of audits was about 2% of the total returns filed.[2] Lately, the picture has improved in favor of the taxpayer. With less than 83,000 employees to process the 95 million returns for 1982, the IRS was able to audit only 1.5% of them.

We can go on looking at statistics for many pages, but that will take us only so far. The most important information for the Guerrilla Capitalist, or any taxpayer, is the dynamics of tax collection; how it works in practice. Only by looking closely at the system is it possible to analyze the weak points and determine how to lessen the tax bite.

The basic process for the taxpayer is this: declare your income, subtract your deductions, and pay tax on the balance. For the purposes of this discussion, we will not differentiate between deductions, exemptions, and tax credits. They all accomplish the same thing — lessen your tax bite.

All of the tax books tell you the same thing: minimize your income and maximize your deductions, in order to pay the least tax.[3,4] This is the conventional wisdom, and it is true. It is what they don't tell you that is even more important to the Guerrilla Capitalist.

The big weakness in the IRS's system for collecting taxes is in *income reporting*. Former IRS Commissioner Jerome Kurtz, in his testimony before Congress[5], says those who earn money in a conventional job, with witholding and W-2 forms, report 97% to 98% of their income. By contrast, those who are self-employed report only 60% to 64% of the total. The chances of concealing income are much greater if you are self-employed than if you work for wages that leave a paperwork trail.

This leads to the most important point of all: in your dealings with the IRS, the burden of proof is upon them regarding your income, but it is upon you regarding your deductions.

While in theory, you are required to list all of your income, they can't make you do it unless they can catch you under-reporting. To take deductions, on the other hand, you must list them and have available the receipts and other paperwork to support them, if you are ever audited. If you cannot prove a deduction, or show that an expenditure falls within the allowable categories, the IRS can and will disallow it.

We can see from this why many wage-earning taxpayers feel the tax burden hits them especially hard. Their employers record and report every cent they make to the government, while others who earn their incomes differently can play games with the IRS and get away with it, if they are discreet.

Wages. With the paperwork trail this sort of income leaves, there are not many chances for anyone to get away with not paying taxes on it. There is one method that is useful only to the person who chooses to live totally "underground." If such a person assumes a totally false identity, with false I.D. papers[6] and lists enough exemptions on his W-4 when he takes a job, he will have very little withheld from his wages. For this to work consistently, the person must be able to move on to a new job each year or two, before the IRS catches up to him.

Illegal immigrants sometimes work a variation of this scheme. They will borrow a relative's Social Security card or fill in a totally false Social Security number on the W-4. They normally live a nomadic existence, and in many cases are caught by the Immigration Service and deported before the IRS can call them in for an audit.

Cash payments. This is the basic form of concealable income. The person who is paid "under the table," or performs services for which he is paid in cash, can easily neglect to report all or part of this income, since cash is untraceable.

Payments by check. Incredibly, many people still get away with underreporting income by check, when it is not wage income. Even though checks leave a definite paperwork trail, and banks microfilm every check they handle, the fact is this information is not available to the IRS unless you are audited. If you are, and the auditor feels your bank records are worth a look, he can subpoena them, and that's the end of the game for you. With only 1.5% of the tax returns being audited, and an even smaller proportion subjected to a close investigation, the odds against this happening are comforting.

Even in this day and age, it is possible to get along without a checking account.[7] It is still perfectly legal to pay your bills in cash, or by money order. It is also legal to have someone else cash your checks for you, if you have a customer who pays you by check. If you are a plumber, for example, and you do a little moonlighting after hours, your supplier may be willing to have you sign over second party checks, if he knows you well.

Rents, royalities, and other income. This is the broadest category of all, and contains many sources of income that are capable of concealment. The IRS is tightening up its controls, now requiring, for example, that a Form 1099 be sent in for many of these payments, but there are still many gaps. Interest on savings is regularly reported by banks, and some tips are now subject to withholding, but rents are not under such tight controls, and income from capital gains on

142

coins, stamps and precious metals are still basically out of reach of the IRS, although it now requires stockbrokers to report their clients' earnings.

NOTES

1. U.S. Treasury Dept. figures as reported in *U.S. News and World Report,* April 18, 1983.

2. *How to Cheat on Your Taxes,* by "X," C.P.A., 1040 Press, p. 91.

3. *Taxpayer's Survival Manual,* Howard Fishkin, Book Promotions Unlimited, P.O. Box 122, Flushing, Mich. 48433.

4. *In This Corner, The IRS,* J.R. Price, 1981, Dell Publishing Co.

5. *Hearings Before The Joint Economic Committee, Congress of the United States, Ninety-Sixth Congress, First Session,* November 15, 1979, pp. 2-3.

6. *The Paper Trip,* and *The New Paper Trip,* Eden Press.

7. *No Checks,* Robert B. Clarkson, 1982, The Constitutionalist Press, PO Box 17001, Greenville, SC 29607.

25

How the I.R.S. Plays "Gotcha"

Anyone who does not pay the taxes the government says he owes runs the risk of being forced to pay or, in extreme cases, criminal prosecution. The IRS fosters a climate of fear by barking a lot, but as we shall see, its bite is not as terrible as some believe.

The first thing to make clear is that the IRS is after your money, not your life or freedom. A taxpayer in prison cannot earn money, and the government, instead of taking part of his earnings, has to pay his room and board. In 1979, only 1,820 people were formally prosecuted for tax evasion.[1] That is a tiny proportion of the people audited, and an even tinier part of all those who evaded taxes and were never caught.

Basically, the IRS requires you to report your own income and tax owed. Sometimes you are locked in, as when you work for wages and your employer withholds taxes and files a W-2 with the IRS. The IRS will pursue non-filers, those who have paperwork indicating income but who fail to file a return themselves. It will also pursue tax rebels who openly proclaim themselves as such.[2]

Many people file tax returns which provoke the IRS to take a closer look at them. The IRS has a checklist, known as the "Discriminant Function System," which they use to pick out returns that are likely to contain major errors or reflect attempts at evasion, enabling them to zero in on people who can be coerced into coughing up more taxes. The Discriminant Function System, or DIF for short, is a list of ways in which tax returns differ from averages the IRS has worked out over the years. It also reflects their experience in picking out certain categories which suggest the filer is concealing something. Some specifics are:

1. Outstanding discrepancies, such as claiming no children one year, and ten the next, or an income that is completely out of line with your occupational category, e.g., they will not believe that a lawyer earns only five thousand dollars a year.

2. Deductions much larger than average. The IRS will want substantiation, or they will disallow it. A table showing some average deductions for different levels of income is useful to every accountant, and necessary to every taxpayer who wants to be on solid ground.[3]

3. Returns showing heavy travel and entertainment deductions. Experience has shown that many abuses occur in these categories.

4. Those claiming exemptions for other dependents besides wives or children.

5. Those which list a hobby as a deduction, claiming it is a business. For this to work, the "business" must occasionally show a "profit."

6. Returns from people who, by the nature of their work, have the greatest opportunities to cheat. This includes not only doctors and lawyers, but anyone else who deals largely in cash.

This last point is worth a close look. A person who earns less than $10,000 a year and is subject to a W-2 form has to face a 1 in 143 chance of being audited.[4] A self-employed person with an income of over $30,000 annually has a 1 in 17 chance of being audited. Someone earning W-2 reportable wages that total over $50,000 a year has a 1 in 9 chance of facing the auditor. At first, this seems inconsistent, but

146

experience has shown that those who are self-employed and deal in cash have the opportunity to conceal income, and that will be the main direction of an audit. Those with large W-2 salaries, on the other hand, are likely to be businessmen who are creative in devising large deductions. The IRS will approach them from a different direction.

The IRS also has a small program of spot-checks, in which returns are selected at random in what it calls the Taxpayers Compliance Measurement Program. This is like being struck by lightning. It probably won't happen to you, but if it does, the auditor will go over every detail of your return, while in a conventional audit he'll question only the areas which have attracted his attention.

The IRS has two methods of auditing the return: direct and indirect. The direct method involves gathering and examining the paperwork related to the return — the W-2, the Form 1040, receipts to support deductions, etc. This is the method it uses to knock down returns that are fudged with inflated deductions.

The indirect method is more sophisticated, and is the one the IRS uses to check on unreported income. IRS investigators can, and do, subpoena bank records, business ledgers, invoices, and other paperwork in order to verify the accuracy of the reported income.

Sometimes it is obvious. A person who owns a yacht and claims income of only $10,000 a year is plainly living beyond his reported means, and will have a lot of explaining to do.

Sometimes it is more subtle. A businessman who claims a rate of profit lower than the norm for his type of enterprise may be concealing income, and the examiner may check his bank records to determine his cash flow, and construct a picture of how it adds up for the year. He may use sophisticated accounting methods, such as deriving a figure for net worth, checking inventory at the start and the end of the year, totaling cash register tapes, etc.[5]

In certain cases, the IRS will open a frontal attack by asking the taxpayer for a cost-of-living statement from him. This lists all of his living expenses, and the examiner will compare the total with the claimed income. This is necessary when the income is really untraceable, and no other method will do.

You, as a citizen and taxpayer, may feel outraged that the IRS can dig into your private records in its search for additional taxes. Nevertheless, it can, and has the law on its side. Bank records, which normally require a court order to make them available to another party, are vulnerable to what is colloquially known as a "pocket summons," which an IRS agent can whip out and fill in on the spot to compel your banker to open your records to him.[6]

The picture is not all black. Although the IRS has some very heavy artillery which it can use, it rarely does so, and if you are wise and keep a low profile, your chances of being bombarded with a full-scale investigation are small.

NOTES

1. *In This Corner, The IRS,* J.R. Price, Dell Publishing, 1981, p. 234.

2. *Inside the Underground Economy,* Jerome Tuccille, New American Library, 1982, pp. 11-43.

3. *How To Cheat On Your Taxes,* "X," C.P.A., 1040 Press, p. 33.

4. *Tax Avoidance,* Anonymous, privately printed, p. 7.

5. *In This Corner, The IRS,* pp. 119-232. These chapters are a comprehensive and excellent discussion of how the IRS proves income. They show the vulnerabilities of those who try to conceal their incomes, and how the IRS takes advantage of them to reveal undeclared income. Reading between the lines suggests ways of strengthening the vulnerabilities and plugging the leaks.

6. *Advanced Investigative Techniques for Private Financial Records*, Richard A. Nossen, Loompanics Unlimited, 1984. This is a manual for government investigators on how to nab citizens for income tax evasion. It discusses in vast detail the types of records your bank maintains on you, and how to reconstruct your financial history from these records.

26

Protecting Yourself
From the I.R.S.

Every Guerrilla Capitalist, if he is wise, will consider the possibility that he may be "called down" by the IRS for an audit or a more extensive investigation. We have already seen that an audit may come about routinely, as part of the Taxpayer Compliance Measurement Program, or it may come because the IRS has noted a feature of your tax return which suggests non-compliance with the tax laws.[1]

The Guerrilla Capitalist who is aware of the possibilities can prepare to meet them, and more importantly, can take steps to avoid them. This is a crucial point. Historically, the guerrilla has been the underdog, too weak to fight the established forces on their own ground. This also applies to the Guerrilla Capitalist. He cannot come out to fight openly against the IRS. If he tries, he'll find the IRS, with the power of the federal government on its side, will usually win.

The basic principle of success in Guerrilla Capitalism is *avoidance is better than confrontation.* That is why it is wise to keep a low profile. There have been some who have ignored this principle and found it very costly. Recently, on the TV program, *Sixty Minutes,* several tax evaders boasted how they had fooled the IRS, possibly without realizing IRS people watch that program, too. The result was predictable.

They all were called down for some uncomfortable sessions with tax examiners.

There have been others. Lucille Moran, a prominent tax protestor, steadfastly refused to file a return for years. This resulted in a running legal battle with the IRS. A man named Irwin Schiff became involved in a long legal struggle with the IRS by filing what has come to be known as a "Fifth Amendment Return," one on which the taxpayer writes his name and address, and the statement that he declines to answer the other questions under the protection of the Fifth Amendment. The IRS sees this as an affront to their authority, and prosecutes those who do this. The tax protestors appeal their convictions,[2] but a long, drawn-out legal contest is inevitably expensive. In any event, on April 19th, 1983, the U.S. Supreme Court ruled that citizens cannot claim Fifth Amendment protection to withhold information from the IRS.[3]

Another open defiance of the IRS is starting a "church," a right guaranteed by the First Amendment of the Constitution.[4] Unfortunately, those who have tried this have found that the IRS is not stupid, and have had to fight legal battles to maintain their status. Again, this is expensive, and even if the protester wins, he might find that it has cost him dearly.

The successful Guerrilla Capitalist wants to *avoid* a fight with the IRS. He does this by keeping a low profile, blending in with millions of other citizens. The analogy of trying to find a needle in a haystack teaches a basic insight regarding how this works. It is difficult to find a needle in a haystack, because it is so small. Yet, it can be done with a metal detector. Finding one particular strand of hay, which looks exactly like millions of others, though, is almost impossible. The Guerrilla Capitalist tries to look just like all of the other strands of hay in the haystack. He does not draw attention to himself by claiming deductions so large they seem unreal. He does not make a spectacle of himself by openly confronting the IRS. He knows for the IRS to harass him, they first have to notice him, and he makes that as unlikely as possible.

We have seen what the IRS looks for in selecting returns for audit. Avoiding the features of such returns is one means of prevention, and we know that prevention is better than cure.

The Guerrilla Capitalist who finds himself called down for an audit can prepare to face that, too, if he keeps his wits about him and informs himself properly before he goes to the IRS office. There is excellent published material on how to handle an audit[5,6]. There is also good advice on what not to do in order to handle an audit properly and avoid the attention of the IRS.

We can quickly go over the basics here:

If you are called for an audit, be prepared, bringing with you all of the documents requested, but no more

During the audit, don't try to bluff or bully the auditor or be overly friendly. It is important to keep in mind these people are pros, and have seen it all before. What might seem to you an ingenious tactic will be old hat to them.

Answer questions simply and directly, but — and this is an important but — don't rush. Think out your answers very carefully before you open your mouth. Some investigators may try to force the pace by snapping questions at you, to induce you to snap an answer back without thinking. Avoid this at all costs, but be open about it. Tell the investigator frankly that you want a minute or so to think about your answer, or you want to look at your receipts to refresh your memory. If you need more time to think, ask to go to the bathroom. That is a request the examiner cannot refuse, and it will buy you several minutes time.

If you are the nervous type, and easily get flustered under pressure, admit your weakness to yourself and have your tax accountant accompany you to the session. You may want to do this anyway, as a routine precaution. Your accountant is a pro, accustomed to dealing with the IRS. The examiner will not be able to bulldoze him as he might an unpracticed and unsophisticated taxpayer. IRS auditors have been known to employ unfair tactics, and try to bluff taxpayers when they feel the taxpayer does not know all his rights.

Be prepared for traps and trick questions. Never forget these examiners interview people all day, every day, and are skilled at drawing out vital information with seemingly trivial questions.[7,8].

It is critically important, and worth repeating, that you must participate in the interview in a careful and deliberate manner, for your own protection.

One of the most common traps is the cost-of-living statement that an examiner will ask a taxpayer to fill out when there is difficulty in finding documentation of his income. This is an indirect method of establishing income, and is loaded with traps. It is in your best interest to minimize your expenditures, for obvious reasons, and you should be very careful with your answers.

All in all, keeping your head down is the best basic tactic. Not giving the IRS reason to investigate you will avoid many problems with them, and if you're called for an audit, giving an impression of being an honest and typical taxpayer will help disarm their suspicions.

NOTES

1. *In This Corner, The IRS,* J.R. Price, Dell Publishing, 1981, p. 54-69.

2. *Inside The Underground Economy,* Jerome Tuccille, New American Library, 1982, pp. 11-48. This is an excellent discussion of the above-ground tax protestors and how the IRS has followed an active campaign against them.

3. *Associated Press,* April 20, 1983.

4. *Churchification: Incorporate Your Own Church Without a Lawyer.* Church Liberation League, 1983.

5. *Taxpayer's Survival Manual,* by Howard Fishkin, 1979, Book Promotions, Unltd., PO Box 122, Flushing, Mich. 48433, pp. 46-49. This is a summary of ways to behave at an audit.

6. *In This Corner, The IRS,* pp. 54-69 and pp.208-231. This material gives an insight into how the IRS sees this issue, and what its objectives are. The author, a former IRS agent, knows his material and gives very detailed information on how the IRS works.

7. *How to Cheat On Your Taxes,* by "X," C.P.A., 1040 Press, pp. 102-103. This is a very good list of "don'ts" for those who want to avoid trouble with the IRS.

8. *Taxpayer's Survival Manual.* Page 49 has a short discussion of traps in the interview.

27

Striking Back:
Guerrilla War Against the I.R.S.

For good reasons, many people feel helpless against the bureaucracy of the government. They may write to the local newspaper, or to their congressman, but in their hearts they know this will do nothing meaningful. They also know if they try to fight the IRS openly, they will get their heads knocked off, or be involved in aggravating litigation that can go on for years.

There are ways of fighting back without being singled out and getting hurt. There are ways to throw monkey wrenches into the complicated machinery of the IRS without becoming a martyr. Let's look at a few of them:

THE ROUTINE WAYS

The IRS operates more and more with computers, in an effort to cope with the mountains of paperwork they must process each year. It also has to work within a budget, with limited resources and manpower to pursue its cases. One consequence of this is that the IRS sends out pre-printed, specially coded envelopes to many taxpayers along with their Form 1040 and booklet. If you get one of these packages, remember the IRS is not providing you with a pre-addressed envelope because they're nice guys. The envelopes are coded to go through a computerized sorting machine, to speed up processing. Returns that come in other envelopes must be sorted by hand, which consumes manpower. Therefore, do not use the envelope or peel-away label the IRS sends you, unless you expect a refund and want to speed up the processing of your return. Make them sort it by hand.

If you have some spare time one day, and are in a good mood, get some Form 1040s and some blank W-2s. Fill them out with fictitious names and send them in. An interesting twist is to use names and addresses of people who have died recently, as seen in the obituary columns. For the accompanying W-2, fill in the name of a real company you have reason to dislike, such as an auto dealer who sold you a lemon. To make sure the return gets their attention, fill it out to show the taxpayer owes money. They will make every effort to track the person down to collect, diverting manpower they otherwise might have used to harass a Guerrilla Capitalist.

IF YOU ARE AUDITED

If you have the misfortune to be selected for audit, you'll probably receive a notice giving you the time and place of the audit, and telling you what documents to bring. This is your golden chance to strike hard, if you are clever.

Keep in mind that the IRS is in operation to collect money, and they have to do this with limited means. Former IRS Commissioner Mortimer Caplin liked to boast that the IRS collected five dollars for every one spent on enforcement of the tax laws. The right tactics can put a crimp in that figure.

Each auditor has to work his way through a heavy caseload, and has to meet a quota. An unofficial estimate is that each auditor has to produce $100 in additional taxes per hour he works. Your goal is to reduce his productivity by wasting his time, which you can do easily if you are smart and discreet about it.

The first step is to phone your assigned auditor to break your appointment, the same day if possible. Tell him you have an emergency (doctor, dentist, car broke down, etc.) and ask if you can meet him at the same time the next day. Show willingness to come in as soon as possible after the original appointment, to maintain the appearance of cooperation.

If you have to lose pay from your job because of this, be sure that you remember that more than a few hours' pay is at stake here. If your boss is a decent fellow, and feels the same way you do about the IRS, he can alibi you for the broken first appointment.

When you do go in, be on time, again to show good faith. It will count against you if you are late, and you may risk being labeled a wise guy. When you meet the auditor, be polite, and don't try any of the cheap tricks they have all encountered before, such as being "buddy-buddy" with him or her, or screaming about your "rights." They are used to this, and will not be impressed. Adopt a low-key manner, and don't antagonize the examiner.

Bring the documents requested with you, but be sure to bring only those requested. Have them arranged neatly, so you can find them quickly. Don't make the mistake of bringing in a shopping bag full of receipts and dumping them on his desk. He has seen that before, too, and if he gets angry with you, he might go after you whatever the cost.

Answer his questions politely, but take your time, as if you are thinking carefully before answering. Remember that he has his appointments closely scheduled, and has only so much time to devote to your case. When he asks you to produce a document, do it, but do it slowly and carefully, without making it obvious you're out to waste his time.

If he asks you to produce a document that was not listed on the form you got (bring the form with you, to show him) say:

"I'm sorry, but you didn't ask for that. If I'd known, I would have brought it."

If he asks you to provide any information that is not dealt with in the documents you have, don't answer it. Tell him you don't remember, but you'll be glad to go home and get your checkbook, rent receipts, etc., and bring them next time.

One technique examiners use is asking the taxpayer to fill out a cost of living sheet, which covers all his expenses for the previous year. This is the golden opportunity to stonewall him, if you do it correctly. Be modest about it, and soft-spoken. For example:

"I don't know exactly what we pay for rent. My wife makes out the checks. I'll be glad to go and get them, though."

If he tells you to give him an estimate, refuse absolutely:

"I can't be sure what I would tell you would be right. I have to sign that paper, and I don't want to risk perjury."

If he tells you that there is no risk of perjury, reply that you would prefer to give him accurate information, and the records to support it are at home. Be tactful, but firm.

Remember you are playing for time, and trying to waste his, and make him work for every penny he squeezes out of you. If you can present yourself as a poor but honest soul, he might even decide there is not much to gain in spending more time on the investigation, and drop it at that point. This may let you off the hook.

If, however, he tries to bulldoze you, and tells you he is going to disallow a certain deduction because you don't have the supporting documents there, dig in your feet. The gloves are off. If you really have the documents at home, insist on speaking to his supervisor. Tell him, politely of course, that you can prove your point and you want to come back with the paperwork. If he tells you to mail them, tell him you have recently lost some important papers in the mail, and you'd prefer to hand-carry them.

These tactics might seem petty, but they will result in wasting the examiner's very limited time. Each hour he

160

spends on you he will not be able to use to pursue another taxpayer. His backlog of cases will continue to pile up. The tax auditors are so overloaded that even a few people practicing delaying tactics will jam up their systems.

28

Recommended Reading

There is not much in print on the underground economy as such — you have to search and read between the lines. The following works are recommended as the best sources of further information.

THE UNDERGROUND ECONOMY

Beating the System: The Underground Economy, by Carl P. Simon and Ann D. Witte. Auburn House Publishing Company, Boston, 1982. This book covers mainly activities which are criminal in themselves, such as cigarette bootlegging, loan sharking, and the like.

The Black Market: A Study of White Collar Crime, by Marshall B. Clinnard. Originally published in 1952, this is a study of the price controls and rationing system in the U.S.A. in WWII, and goes into considerable detail as to exactly how the controls were evaded by the population.

Black Markets Around the World, by Burgess Laughlin. Loompanics Unlimited, 1981. Articles on various illegal markets around the world, from the labor market in the Netherlands, to apartments in Sweden, to illegal vegetables in Canada.

Estimates of Income Unreported on Individual Tax Returns. Internal Revenue Service Publication 1104(9-79). Government report dealing with the "problem" of unreported income.

The Justice Times, Box 562, Clinton, AR 72031. Monthly tabloid covering the aboveground tax protest movement.

Job Opportunities in the Black Market, by Burgess Laughlin. Loompanics Unlimited, 1981. This book is an underground classic. It is an in-depth study of the illegal, but victimless economy in the United States. The single best book on illegal economic activities ever written.

Laissez Faire Books, Inc., 206 Mercer St., New York, NY 10012. The best source of books on free market economics — comprehensive selection and good service.

National Taxpayers Union, 325 Pennsylvania Ave., S.E., Washington, D.C. 20003. An excellent source of facts, figures, and information on overtaxing and overspending by the U.S. Government.

New Libertarian Manifesto, by Samuel E. Konkin III. Koman Publishing, PO Box 10427, Marina del Ray, CA 90291. Lays out the theoretical basis for underground economic activities and the development of counter-economic institutions.

The Subterranean Economy, by Dan Bawly. McGraw-Hill, 1982. This is the best "mainstream" book on the underground economy, not only in the United States, but in other countries as well. The author states flat out that inept government, inflation and taxation are what creates underground economies. Really worth reading.

The Underground Economy. Hearing before the Joint Economic Committee, 96th Congress, First Session, November 15, 1979. Available from U.S. Government Printing Office, Washington, DC 20402. Mostly bureaucratic drivel, but there is some useful information in here.

The Underground Economy in the United States and Abroad, edited by Vito Tanzi. Lexington Books, 1982. *Very* dry and scholarly, but covers a lot of ground.

STARTING NEW BUSINESSES
AND MOONLIGHTING

Armchair Millionaire, by Fred Hal Vice. Paladin Press, PO Box 1307, Boulder, CO 80306, 1981. A decent book on starting your own business.

The Complete Book of International Smuggling, by M.C. Finn, Paladin Press, 1983. Not all smuggling involves high-risk items like guns or dope. A decent living can be made bringing in low-risk items. This book covers the big time smuggling scene.

Contracting Out: The Employer's Survival Employment System. Business Practical Consultants, Inc., PO Box 15567, Phoenix, AZ 85060, 1978. Tells small businessmen how to turn their employees into sub-contractors, with considerable savings in taxes for both parties.

Duty Free: Smuggling Made Easy, by Michael Connor. Paladin Press, 1983. A how-to-do-it handbook on smuggling whatever you want through Customs.

Government By Emergency, by Gary North. American Bureau of Economic Research, PO Box 8204, Ft. Worth, TX 76112, 1983. This book contains the essay "Inflation and the Return of the Craftsman," one of the most intelligent pieces we have seen on choosing a career in inflation-ridden times. North also publishes a newsletter, *Remnant Review,* which often contains excellent advice on coping with and evading bureaucracy.

How I Found Freedom In An Unfree World, by Harry Browne. Avon Books, 1973. The single best "breaking free" book ever written. Full of practical advice on getting yourself free from government, jealousy, exploitation, the rat race, etc. I can't recommend this one highly enough.

How to Become a Modern Day Gold Prospector, American Association of Jewelry Brokers, PO Box 6954, Tyler, TX 75711, 1984. Mistitled — this is *not* about prospecting out in the desert — it is about buying scrap gold and reselling it.

Published as a companion to *Secrets of Diamond Dealing* (opposite page). Very practical and useful.

How to Convert Your Favorite Hobby, Sport, Pastime or Idea to Cash, by Al Riolo. Business Development and Research Center, PO Box 5499, Sacramento, CA 95817, 1983. Good advice on making a business of your hobby.

How to Earn $15 to $50 an Hour & More with a Pick-Up Truck or Van, by Don Lilly. Darian Books, RD 1, Canal Road, Princeton, NJ 08540, 1982. Very practical book on making money hauling.

How to Hustle Home Poker, by John Fox. GBC Press, Box 4115, Las Vegas, NV 89106, 1981. An excellent manual on making money in home poker games.

In Search of Gold, by Stephen M. Voynick. Paladin Press, 1982. This one is about finding gold outdoors, and covers every possible way and place. Panning, rock mining, treasure hunting, beachcombing, artifact excavating, and even graverobbing!

Increase Your Take-Home Pay Up To 40%, by Ted Nicholas. Enterprise Publishing, Inc., 725 Market St., Wilmington, DE 19801. Same subject as *Contracting Out* (previous page), but written from the employee's viewpoint, rather than the employer's.

Make Money By Moonlighting: Own Your Own Low-Risk Business, by Jack Lander. Enterprise Publishing, Inc. 1982. Excellent book on starting up a part-time business.

Making Money With Your Microcomputer, by Robert J. Traister & Rich Ingram. TAB Books, Blue Ridge Summit, PA 17214, 1982. Just what the title says.

Money Is My Friend, by Phil Laut. Trinity Publications, 1636 N. Curson Ave., Hollywood, CA 90046, 1979. Good book about mastering money, instead of money mastering you.

Moonlighting: A Complete Guide to Over 200 Exciting Part-Time Jobs, by Peter-Davidson. McGraw-Hill, 1983. Just what the title says.

Poker: A Guaranteed Income for Life Using the Advanced Concepts of Poker, by Frank R. Wallace. The definitive book on making money in home poker games. Very ruthless and practical.

Secrets of Diamond Dealing. Now available through D & G Direct, PO Box 1084, Whitehouse, TX 75791. The definitive manual on speculating in diamonds.

The Seven Laws of Money, by Michael Phillips. Random House, 1974. An excellent book on money and your relationship to it and its relationship to you.

Shortcuts to a Fortune in Appliance Repair, by Frank M. Cassaday. Cassaday Enterprises, 3452 Rolls Beach Dr., San Diego, CA 92111, 1981. An excellent manual on starting an appliance repair business. Good opportunity!

Sneak It Through: Smuggling Made Easier, by Michael Connor. Paladin Press, 1984. More on smuggling techniques by the author of *Duty Free* (page 165).

Underground Car Dealer, by Maxwell DeSoto. Underground Reports, 4418 East Chapman Ave., Ste. 144, Orange, CA 92669, 1983. Blueprint for an underground used car business.

FLEA MARKETS, CONVENTIONS, GARAGE AND YARD SALES

The Complete Guide to Gun Shows, by Thomas W. Thielen. Loompanics Unlimited, 1980. Just what the title says — contains a wealth of information on buying and selling at gun shows, and even how to put on your own gun show.

The Complete Guide to Science Fiction Conventions, by Erwin S. Strauss. Loompanics Unlimited, 1983. Good book on how SF cons are run, including dealer rooms.

Don't Throw It Out — Sell It, by Joe Sutherland Gould. Prentice-Hall, 1983. Good book on selling used goods through garage sales, flea markets, second-hand stores, etc.

Farmers Markets of America: A Renaissance, by Robert Sommer. Capra Press, PO Box 2068, Santa Barbara, CA 93120. Farmers markets, roadside stands, etc.

Flea Market America, by Cree McCree. John Muir Publications, Inc., PO Box 613, Santa Fe, NM 87501. Flea markets, garage sales, etc. Includes a chapter on selling.

Flea Market Handbook, by Robert G. Miner. Main Street Books, Mechanicsburg, PA 17055, 1981. Excellent book on selling at flea markets. Full of practical advice.

How to Make More Money with Your Garage Sale, by Ryan Petty. St. Martin's Press, 1981. Good advice on getting the most out of garage and yard sales.

Success Is Not Working for the Pharoah: An Introduction to High Yield Cottage Industry, by Steve and Cindy Long. Idahome Publications, 9395 Rapid Lightning Road, Sandpoint, ID 83864. An excellent book on running a craft business, and how to set up and sell at shows, etc. Written by a couple who actually earn their livings this way, it is full of valuable tips and information.

Successful Flea Market Selling, by Valerie Bohigian. TAB Books, 1981. Worthwhile book on flea markets and how to sell at them.

BARTER

The Barter Book, by Dyanne Asimow Simon. Doubleday, 1979. This is the single finest book on barter ever written. The author is very sympathetic with the tax evasion aspects of barter.

The Barter Way to Beat Inflation, by George W. Burtt. Everest House, 1980. Covers the possibilities of barter, but with way too much emphasis on barter clubs and exchanges.

Fundamentals of Successful Bartering, by Ron Levy. Koala Press, Santa Barbara, CA 1982. Good tips on haggling, but the author recommends barter exchanges.

Let's Try Barter, by Charles Morrow Wilson. Devin-Adair Co., 143 South Beach Ave., Old Greenwich, CT 06870, 1976. Probably the best book on barter, next to *The Barter Book* (opposite page).

Survival Bartering, by Duncan Long. Long Survival Publications, PO Box 163, Wamego, KS 66547, 1981. Treats barter in an "after the crash" situation.

THE I.R.S., TAXES, AND FIDDLING THE BOOKS

Advanced Investigative Techniques for Private Financial Records, by Richard A. Nossen. Loompanics Unlimited, 1984. A manual for tax agents on how to snoop into your financial records and uncover unreported income. Very comprehensive and thorough. Also very scary. Must reading for all Guerrilla Capitalists.

Clarkson's No Checks, by Robert B. Clarkson. Constitutionalist Press, PO Box 17001, Greenville, SC 29607, 1982. Booklet by a tax protestor on how to avoid checks, how to use non-reproducing blue pens to evade bank microfilming of checks, etc.

How to Cheat on Your Taxes, by "X," C.P.A. 1040 Press, 1983. Exactly what the title says — a book that has been needed for years. Very well done, and should be read by all Guerrilla Capitalists.

How to Obtain a Fair Trial, by Eugene Wilson. J.C. Printing Co., 3493 N. Main St., College Park, GA 30337, 1983. Covers how to handle yourself if the IRS brings criminal charges against you. Written by a lawyer.

In This Corner, the IRS, by J.R. Price. Dell Publishing, 1981. Includes a good section on how the IRS discovers unreported income.

IRS In Action, by Santo M. Presti. Bristol Publishing Co., Fairport, NY, 1983. Good book about how the IRS operates, written by a former treasury agent.

The Mirage, by Zay N. Smith and Pamela Zekman. Random House, 1979. One of the most interesting books ever written. A team of investigative reporters opened a bar in Chicago and recorded all the corruption, bribes, shakedowns, and tax evasion schemes they encountered. Fascinating reading!

Taxpayer's Survival Manual, by Howard Fishkin. Book Promotions Unlimited, PO Box 122, Flushing, MI 48433. Interesting book on dealing with the IRS, written by a professional tax preparer.

When You Owe the IRS, by Jack Warren Wade, Jr. Macmillan, 1983. What to do when the IRS comes after your goods.

Write-Off! Tax Tips H & R Block Won't Give You, by Joan Flynn. Article in *High Times* Magazine, April, 1980. High Times, 17 W. 60th St., New York, NY 10023. Article on tax evasion, with particular attention to concealing assets, keeping a low profile, and laundering money. Written especially for dope dealers, but useful for any Guerrilla Capitalist.

UNDERGROUND INVESTING

The Alpha Strategy, by John A. Pugsley. Stratford Press, 1981. An excellent book on investing in real goods, instead of paper stocks, etc. Good advice on stockpiling and hoarding. Must reading for all Guerrilla Capitalists.

Crisis Preparedness Handbook, by Jack A. Spigarelli. Resource Publications, PO Box 151, Provo, UT 84603, 1984. A comprehensive guide to home storage of food and emergency supplies. What to store and how to do it.

How to Bury Your Goods, by Eddie the Wire. Loompanics Unlimited, 1981. The most comprehensive manual ever written on long-term underground storage. For hardcore individualists.

How to Hide Anything, by Michael Connor. Paladin Press, 1984. Excellent book on hiding things inside and outside of your home.

How to Launder Money, by John Gregg. Loompanics Unlimited, 1982. How the big boys do it. Using offshore corporations and tax havens, investing money without reporting it to the IRS, etc.

The Survival Retreat, by Ragnar Benson. Paladin Press, 1983. Very practical and down-to-earth book on putting together a safe place, well worth reading.

Survivalist's Medicine Chest, by Ragnar Benson. Paladin Press, 1982. How to stockpile medicines, with emphasis on buying them cheap.

DODGING BIG BROTHER

The Code Book: All About Unbreakable Codes and How to Use Them, by Michael E. Marotta. Loompanics Unlimited, 1983. How to conceal information. A second set of books, directions to buried goods, whatever secrets you want to keep.

Directory of Mail Drops in the United States and Canada, compiled by Michael Hoy. Loompanics Unlimited, 1983. More than 700 places around the world where you can rent an unlisted address and have mail forwarded to you wherever you want.

How to Get I.D. in Canada And Other Countries, by Ronald George Eriksen 2. Loompanics Unlimited, 1984. Step-by-step instructions for obtaining alternative ID in Canada and other foreign countries.

I.D. For Sale: A Comprehensive Guide to the Mail Order I.D. Industry, by Michael Hoy. Loompanics Unlimited, 1983. All kinds of I.D. cards you can order through the mail. Useful for extra bank accounts, etc.

Methods of Disguise, by John Sample. Loompanics Unlimited, 1984. Everything you ever wanted to know about changing your appearance.

New I.D. in America, by Anonymous. Paladin Press, 1983. Everything there is to know about getting extra ID in America.

The Paper Trip I and *The Paper Trip II,* by Barry Reid. Eden Press, PO Box 8410, Fountain Valley, CA 92708. The classic and original books on getting alternative identification papers.

Privacy: How to Get It; How to Enjoy It, by Bill Kaysing. Eden Press, 1977. A fine book on how to live your life in privacy from Big Brother.

Privacy Journal, PO Box 15300, Washington, DC 20003. Monthly newsletter on all aspects of privacy invasion, corporate as well as government.

YOU WILL ALSO WANT TO READ:

☐ **JOB OPPORTUNITIES IN THE BLACK MARKET,** *by Burgess Laughlin.* The "black" market is the *real* market driven underground by government regulation. This classic book (now in its 6th printing) is the best book available on the illegal, but victimless, economy. Covers pay, organizations, risks, advancement, culture, society, prices and benefits, as well as retailers, wholesalers, middlemen, entrepreneurs, and their assistants. Everything from drugs, sex and people-smuggling to gambling and milk bootlegging. If it's *black market*, it's in this book! *5½ x 8½, 144 pp, illustrated, soft cover,* $10.95. (Order Number 13018)

☐ **How To Do Business "OFF THE BOOKS",** *by Adam Cash.* In *Guerrilla Capitalism*, Adam Cash showed you exactly how millions of Americans are defending themselves against a greedy government by evading taxes, now he digs even deeper into the secrets of the Underground Economy with this amazing new book. *1986, 5½ x 8½, 156 pp, soft cover.* $10.95. (Order Number 13056)

☐ **ADVANCED INVESTIGATIVE TECHNIQUES FOR PRIVATE FINANCIAL RECORDS,** *by Richard A. Nossen.* This manual is used to teach IRS agents how to snoop into *your* private financial records and nail *you* for tax evasion! Includes: Checking and savings accounts; Safe deposit boxes; Cashier's and travelers checks; Bank loan files; Brokerage accounts; Credit card records; Real property holdings; Major cash purchases; And Much More! Learn what you need to do to protect your financial privacy! *1983, 8½ x 11, 86 pp, illustrated, soft cover,* $10.00. (Order Number 13032)

And much more! We offer the very finest in controversial and unusual books — please turn to the catalog announcement on the next page.

Loompanics Unlimited, PO Box 1197, P. Townsend, WA 98368

Please send me the books I have checked above. I am enclosing $_____ (including $2.00 for shipping and handling).

Name_____

Address _____

City/State/Zip_____

We use UPS delivery (unless otherwise requested) if you give us a street address.

"Yes, there are books about the skills of apocalypse — spying, surveillance, fraud, wiretapping, smuggling, self-defense, lockpicking, gunmanship, eavesdropping, car chasing, civil warfare, surviving jail, and dropping out of sight. Apparently writing books is the way mercenaries bring in spare cash between wars. The books are useful, and it's good the information is freely available (and they definitely inspire interesting dreams), but their advice should be taken with a salt shaker or two and all your wits. A few of these volumes are truly scary. Loompanics is the best of the Libertarian suppliers who carry them. Though full of 'you'll-wish-you'd-read-these-when-it's-too-late' rhetoric, their catalog is genuinely informative."

—THE NEXT WHOLE EARTH CATALOG

THE BEST BOOK CATALOG IN THE WORLD!!!

We offer hard-to-find books on the world's most unusual subjects. Here are a few of the topics covered IN DEPTH in our exciting new catalog:

- *Hiding/concealment of physical objects! A complete section of the best books ever written on hiding things!*

- *Fake ID/Alternate Identities! The most comprehensive selection of books on this little-known subject ever offered for sale! You have to see it to believe it!*

- *Investigative/Undercover methods and techniques! Professional secrets known only to a few, now revealed to you to use! Actual police manuals on shadowing and surveillance!*

- *And much, much more, including Locks and Locksmithing, Self-Defense, Intelligence Increase, Life Extension, Money-Making Opportunities, and more!*

Our book catalog is 8½ x 11, packed with over 500 of the most controversial and unusual books ever printed! You can order every book listed! Periodic supplements to keep you posted on the LATEST titles available!!! Our catalog is free with the order of any book on the previous page — or is $3.00 if ordered by itself.

Our book catalog is truly THE BEST BOOK CATALOG IN THE WORLD! Order yours today — you will be very pleased, we know.

LOOMPANICS UNLIMITED
PO BOX 1197
PORT TOWNSEND, WA 98368
USA